Also by Saratoga Ocean

Global Vision: Expanding Business, Trade, and Commerce into Global Awareness

The Final Elimination of the Source of Fear

A GUIDE FOR LIGHTWORKERS
BY ARCHANGEL MICHAEL

SARATOGA OCEAN

Copyright © 2016 Saratoga Ocean.

All rights reserved. No part of this book may be used or reproduced by any means, graphic, electronic, or mechanical, including photocopying, recording, taping or by any information storage retrieval system without the written permission of the publisher except in the case of brief quotations embodied in critical articles and reviews.

Balboa Press books may be ordered through booksellers or by contacting:

Balboa Press
A Division of Hay House
1663 Liberty Drive
Bloomington, IN 47403
www.balboapress.com
1 (877) 407-4847

Because of the dynamic nature of the Internet, any web addresses or links contained in this book may have changed since publication and may no longer be valid. The views expressed in this work are solely those of the author and do not necessarily reflect the views of the publisher, and the publisher hereby disclaims any responsibility for them.

The author of this book does not dispense medical advice or prescribe the use of any technique as a form of treatment for physical, emotional, or medical problems without the advice of a physician, either directly or indirectly. The intent of the author is only to offer information of a general nature to help you in your quest for emotional and spiritual well-being. In the event you use any of the information in this book for yourself, which is your constitutional right, the author and the publisher assume no responsibility for your actions.

Cover art by Marius Michael-George

Artwork © Marius Michael-George – www.Mariusfineart.com

Print information available on the last page.

ISBN: 978-1-4525-9815-4 (sc)
ISBN: 978-1-4525-9817-8 (hc)
ISBN: 978-1-4525-9816-1 (e)

Library of Congress Control Number: 2014919680

Balboa Press rev. date: 3/25/2016

To our beloved planet Earth and all of her inhabitants

CONTENTS

Preface ix
Acknowledgments xiii

Part 1: (Saratoga)
Introduction: A Context for Planetary Evolution 3
Chapter 1: Choices..9
Chapter 2: From Where Does the Heart Derive Its Knowledge? 19
Chapter 3: What about Fear? 29
Chapter 4: Imagination..37
Chapter 5: Inspiration..47
Chapter 6: Heaven 55
Chapter 7: Prosperity 65
Chapter 8: Who You Are in the Universe.............................77
Chapter 9: Into the Light...87

Part 2: (Archangel Michael)
Chapter 10: The Nature of the Universe...............................99
Chapter 11: Prayer...107
Chapter 12: Adam and Eve 113
Chapter 13: Transhumanism 121
Chapter 14: The Angelic Kingdom.....................................131
Chapter 15: The Ego 139

Chapter 16: The Purpose of Life 147
Chapter 17: The Body 157
Chapter 18: The Heart 169
Chapter 19: The Source of Fear 177
Chapter 20: Conclusion 189
Chapter 21: Light 197

Epilogue 203
About the Author 205

PREFACE

The purpose in writing this book is to offer you an opportunity to step back from some of our ancient human assumptions about life on our beloved planet Earth. After thousands of years of human life on this planet, there still remain many unanswered questions of a deeply profound nature. The most fundamental of these questions has to do with the nature of God. If God is Love, then why is there suffering? This question has posed a dilemma that has never been successfully reconciled in our run-of-the-mill, ordinary way of looking at things. The best that we have come up with is to make excuses for God as to why Love would produce suffering in the first place. But what if our assumptions that God created suffering are wrong? What if our entire paradigm is erroneous?

More than twenty-five years ago, I "walked in" to this physical body when the person who inhabited it from birth completed her life and was ready to move on. Such things are only enacted by prior agreement and occur solely through the will of God. It is not possible to produce such an occurrence by one's volition alone. I bring this up because I was able to remain conscious of where I had been before coming to Earth. Earth exists in a wider dimension of reality that we call finite. There are certain characteristics of this finite reality. One of the main characteristics is that things are known by virtue of what they are not rather than by what they are. This is one of the main reasons why we perceive that God is "out there" rather than that which lives in our hearts and is part of who we are. This perception is the root cause of our separation.

In the pages of this book, you will discover an opportunity to view life in a very different way. This opportunity will not come to you because we offer you a new belief system or a new set of so-called facts. Rather, it will come to you as you read the words written first by myself in part 1, and then by Archangel Michael in part 2. The words will envelop you in the form of a process and will open new doorways of perception into your own consciousness. The doors that will open are the doorways that lead to your own divine heart.

We recommend that you read this book from cover to cover if you wish to receive the full benefit of the process contained within. These benefits will not necessarily pertain to your rational, thinking mind. You are probably already very well skilled in the use of your conscious, thinking mind and likely do not need any help in that department. There are already plenty of books written that can provide you with as much input as you could possibly want for the thinking, conceptual mind. We aim to communicate directly with your heart, the seat of your divine intelligence. It is not that this heart requires more information. On the contrary, what the heart really wants is to be heard.

Why is this important? Because the heart exists as your only true doorway to the ultimate truth. No one can tell you in words what this truth is. Our finite, planetary words have no means by which to describe something that completely transcends this reality. We are here to encourage you to embark on your own personal journey of reflection, whereby you seek the counsel of your own heart and your own connection to God and the Universe.

Archangel Michael and I wrote this book together through something similar to automatic writing. I wrote my part, completely inspired by him. He wrote his part through the use of my physical hands at the keyboard. We hope to take you on a journey that weaves between the words since, ironically, the words are not the real point of this communication. You can view the words as mere stepping-stones into a greater reality where those very same words will ultimately be left behind.

Namasté, and enjoy the journey!

ACKNOWLEDGMENTS

I would like to acknowledge the beautiful souls who consider themselves to be lightworkers. They are no doubt the ones responsible for the fact that this book has come into existence. Through their heartfelt and sincere desire to find their true purpose in life, and to help this Earth by enacting that purpose, they have likely drawn this communication forth from Archangel Michael in order to aid their efforts and fully support their love for this planet.

I also want to acknowledge the many angelic beings of Light, who consistently offer their help throughout our Universe as an extension of the Infinite Love of God, and who would do whatever it takes to help us restore ourselves and our planet to a rightful place of harmonious existence in the Universe. All they need is for us to ask. Their dedication and their unwavering love lights the way for all. They remind us that we are never alone and that we are always loved.

PART 1
(Saratoga)

INTRODUCTION

A Context for Planetary Evolution

The purpose of this book is to invite you to question the nature of our existence here on planet Earth. This is a very different approach from looking for ways to cope with our situation as we know it now and to somehow improve our lives by changing things around. We wish to offer you the opportunity for a complete paradigm shift in terms of how you see the world and your life within it.

The benefit in making such a quantum shift lies in a clear understanding of context. Context begets results. If you are currently dissatisfied with the results that you see in your own life and in the world around you, then perhaps a massive perceptual change is in order. If you feel that you have done everything in your power to manifest what you desire, and to assist others in the same, but you feel acutely aware that more is needed, then a new look at your perspective might be necessary.

The massive level of shift in perspective that we are referring to is not something instantly done, particularly when the current perception of life on Earth is as old as the Earth itself. The danger lies in settling for this idea as merely a change in belief systems. For that reason, this book is not written in a typical linear fashion. It is not written for the mind. Instead, this communication is written solely for the heart.

Entering into the communication contents of this writing is in actuality entering into a process. The process requires no effort other than to read. Our English language, and for that matter, all Earth-based languages, are wholly inadequate as a medium through which to convey what it is that you most need to know. Why is that? It is because all of our languages have arisen out of our collective experiences of the problem itself. Which problem are we speaking of? The problem can ultimately be best described in the form of a question: Why is life on Earth so difficult, and why is it that our problems can seem so intractable on an individual and global scale?

Our languages are very good at describing the problem, but they completely fail us when looking for the solution. The best our linear languages can do for us is to provide ideas that weave through our universe of problems in an attempt to help us learn to cope.

Coping is not evolution. It may seem to be at times, particularly if we see a temporary and partial improvement. But in the larger picture overall, whatever gains are made in one person's life or even in one part of the world can be quickly overshadowed by a failure somewhere else. We wish to show you a perspective that is inclusive of all. This perspective reaches across all time and space and spans every single notion of past, present, and future. There is nothing that is left out.

Because language alone cannot serve as a viable communication tool for this, this book is energetically imbued with communication from a much higher order. It is a communication designed to spark insight and

A Context for Planetary Evolution

inspiration long after you have put this book down. It is communication designed to awaken rather than solely to inform.

In order to understand planetary evolution, it is imperative to also understand the context from which you view it. In this process, we will examine that context thoroughly. Some might say that a planetary context is not really relevant to the separate issues in one person's life, but when that planetary context is precisely what gives rise to the possibility of those issues, then it is worth examining.

We, as human beings, are used to knowing things in the exact same way that we always have. Our consciousness is not very flexible in this regard. Science is a perfect example of this. Science attempts to understand the entire cosmos from the same level of knowing that is common to the past, when we didn't know what we are seeking to know now. A scientific breakthrough is really about a breakthrough in perspective. It generally occurs when all other perspectives have been exhausted.

So the question for us now, on an evolutionary scale, is whether we have exhausted all of our previous perspectives about life on this planet as a whole. In our opinion, the answer is yes. Why do we say this? Because in spite of all of our technological advancements, human beings are still human by nature. The same problems persist and continue to worsen. The struggle to have a good or a better life still requires an effort of immense proportions. Our collective sense of guilt causes us to believe that this struggle is deserved.

The points made in this book will not necessarily be made in the way you might be accustomed to, where all of the writing flows in the familiarity of linear thought. Instead, you will see the same things said in different parts of the book, cloaked in similar words, but approaching your consciousness from new and different angles. Why is this necessary? Because the linear, thinking mind is very used to consuming information and processing that information in a way that fits in with what it already knows. To the linear, thinking mind,

A plus B must always equal C. If the mind succeeds in processing this equation, then it will absorb that information and personalize it as a new or compatible belief. If the mind is not successful, then it will automatically discard the information as irrelevant or erroneous. Either one of these scenarios will not serve the purpose for which this communication is intended.

Because of the way in which the linear mind operates, it stands as an ever-present sentry to new and expanded experiences or revelations. It is extremely reluctant to accept that which it cannot effectively process in an old way. It gets around this reluctance by framing new information as a belief. This produces a layering effect, where new information is simply layered on top of old. Have you ever felt that you are carrying around a virtual cartload of all of the different spiritual beliefs that you have been exposed to?

For this reason, this communication has been carefully crafted to bypass all of the mind's filters. So if you find yourself during the course of your reading saying things like, "Why are they repeating that again?" you should know first of all that we are not repeating it. In fact, there is an entirely different communication coming through. The English language is virtually devoid of any words or concepts to express the true meaning of what we may be needing to get across in that moment. There may be literally no words available to reach your consciousness in that particular way. So the communication can be embedded in certain words or concepts that you may have read before, yet they are reaching your consciousness from an entirely different angle.

This is important because your consciousness is by no means one-dimensional. Nor is it limited to linear thought. In other words, you are much, much more than your linear, thinking mind. We wish to communicate with the *whole* you, not just the conscious, thinking part.

It is important that we link this communication to the infinite you, in order to assist you in bringing that infinite self more and more into your conscious awareness. This is the real self that possesses all creative power, insight, and love. This is the self that knows the full truth. So we are not necessarily interested in imparting information only to that part of you that is already full with ordinary input. We are interested in communicating directly with your heart, the seat of your true intelligence. We would like to aid you in opening the door of your divinity so that the intelligence of that divinity can imbue your conscious mind.

Your evolution is part and parcel to planetary evolution. Humanity is a highly significant life form on this planet. We have seen the ability of human beings to destroy when they exist in a wholly misguided state. What we most need to see now is our ability to act as creators and cocreators in this Universe, in a condition where we reach only for Love.

This is where the term *lightworker* has meaning. A lightworker refers to anyone who reaches for the light and reaches for the truth, which can only exist as a manifestation of love. Anyone can be a lightworker, whether or not they subscribe to such a terminology. The word is not important. What matters is the spirit of the heart. Simply being a heart-centered person is the same as being a lightworker. Just *wanting* to be that is also the same thing. Intention is really the key definition. If you intend good for yourself, for this beautiful planet Earth, and for all life forms who live upon it, then you are indeed a lightworker. And your presence is exceedingly important to the welfare and evolution of everyone and everything on Earth.

A lightworker is someone who works for the light. What this means more literally is one who works *toward* the light. One who reaches for love, much as a flower reaches for the sun. Love is a radiant energy that expands, just as light does. Love bathes all whom it touches in serenity, peace, tranquility, and harmony. This is indeed what our collective human soul longs for. We long for peace. We long for the certainty that love provides. We long to be free of conflict and confusion. We long for the freedom and the knowledge to create, and to be our unbridled, godlike selves, without the hesitation that fear demands of us.

Let us consider putting this millennia-old chapter of pain and suffering to a close on our beloved Earth. It is time to return to the real world and to who we really are.

CHAPTER 1

Choices

We are here to offer you a contextual choice as to how you view the evolution of planet Earth. Context is vitally important since it produces its own array of possible results. So the question to ask is, what results are you looking for as a lightworker? We must ask ourselves this question so that we know which direction we wish to take. The direction that we take must always start with a consciously chosen context.

What in our being is responsible for this choice? Well, there are two main options. We can either go with our heads or go with our hearts. To keep it simple, the head refers to the conscious mind, which frequently acts as the voice of the ego, judgment, and past experiences. The heart exists as our connection to Omnipresent Love.

The ego only knows about things that have happened so far, and from this, it derives what it believes to be the current range of opportunities and possible outcomes. The heart exists as our connection to God, Love, and the One who has created all that is. From which source do you believe we are most likely to have access to the greatest possible outcome for all?

To be clear about this subject is of quintessential importance since it is the place from which our prayers and intentions for Earth and all living beings, including ourselves, emerge. So let us take a moment to examine our possibilities from either place.

Let us start with the ego or the head, which is the thinking, conscious mind. The first thing to know about the ego is that it likes to begin with a belief that it knows everything that there is to know in any given moment. It generally rationalizes this position by using past events to shore up its current belief systems. It will happily use the entire known history of planet Earth to justify any position it may take. For example, if the entire known history of Earth includes a never-ending succession of violent events, disease, pain, and suffering, the ego will immediately tell you that that is what you have to work with in terms of context. In other words, the ego will say that such things have always been around, and therefore the idea would be to do the best you can to work around such happenings and find some way to have a happy life. Definitely, this would be an improvement on the situation, and therein lies the rub with relying only upon the ego and the conscious mind. With the ego, you will only receive ideas to improve upon what already exists.

The heart, on the other hand, is already connected to all of creation, whether we are consciously aware of that or not. The heart is who we are in an infinite state, and therefore all knowingness is available from that place. Yet because we as a species are in the habit of relying upon our conscious, thinking minds to evaluate the validity of the heart's messages and intent, we exist and function in sort of a backward state where the factor of inferior knowledge (the mind) controls our awareness of the factor that is connected to infinite knowledge (the heart).

This is vitally important to recognize because it can explain why our world continues to go in circles, where history repeats itself again and again with no appreciable change in our evolutionary status as a world, a species, or a planet. In fact, at the current time, things appear to be getting much worse. This statement should not be construed as negative thinking. It is merely an observation.

So in order to address the matter of context, we must first reckon with our basic alignment of consciousness in terms of what is controlling what. As long as we continue to allow the ego and its voice of the thinking mind to be the deciding force as to how we perceive our condition on planet Earth, we may find some improvement, but the battle will never end.

The ego loves a good battle—especially the battle of good versus evil. That exists as the holy grail for the ego. It can remain energized and alive for untold eons in fighting that battle, and so far it has. The New Age, metaphysical world is filled with good ideas for how to win that battle, as are all religions that have ever been created on this planetary sphere. Religions have tried killing off all of the offenders, and that hasn't worked very well, has it? Especially since new ones are being born every day.

The New Age has sought to elevate that concept by bringing in love and light to all parties involved so as to eventually override those forces of darkness that would happily continue with all of this bad behavior. But either way you look at it, it is still a battle of which side wins out. Given this perspective of duality, the battle will never end. So the context that is commonly held, and rarely questioned, is that there are two sides, and each side hopes to win out over the other. In this scenario, the darkness wants to win as much as the light does.

We collectively come up with all sorts of metaphors to make ourselves feel better, such as "light always dispels the darkness." This may be true in the physical world, but it doesn't work at all in the real world of Omnipresent Love. And why not? Because in that real world, there is no such thing as darkness. There is no battle, and there never was. The battle is simply an illusion. So if our perception rests inside of this illusion, then our solutions will be equally illusionary, no matter how good our intentions. Thus, you have thousands of years of failed attempts to make any appreciable, collective difference.

Now there are many who will argue that this could not possibly be true since there have been all sorts of social, spiritual, and technological improvements around the world. But stand back for a moment and look at the whole. Has violence diminished in any way? Has war abated? How about starvation and poverty? And most importantly, do pain, suffering, and death still exist? And what indeed is the condition of Earth's ecosystems and her natural beauty? Have we ever seen the likes of so much human-made destruction on this planet in its entire history? Of course not.

The ego's context for planetary evolution looks like this: whatever forces and conditions currently exist must have been created by God. The Ultimate Creator must have made this happen, or it wouldn't be here, right? This could be a logical conclusion if your perspective is limited to the thinking mind, the past, and everything that is already known so far on Earth. So we blindly accept the ego's supposition, no questions asked. From here, we collectively form our context from which we pray, hold our intentions, and determine our actions. The only problem is it isn't working!

The heart knows something very different. It knows that death, pain, and suffering should not exist. That is without question as far as the heart is concerned. So what is the context from which this knowing emerges? Well, it is difficult to discuss context as we understand it in a Universe of Infinite Love. Let us start in a very simple way. God is love. Period. There are no compromises or exceptions to this fact.

However, the ego makes a huge exception right off the bat, doesn't it? It wants you to believe that God is love *except* for the experience of pain, suffering, death, and grief. Yet before you have a moment to say,

"Wait a second, that doesn't make any sense!" the ego already has an answer for you. It immediately proceeds to justify its statement with its own peculiar brand of rationale.

"You see," says the ego, "God made all of this suffering, pain, etc., so that we could learn something from it." And before you have a moment to ask, "Learn what, pray tell?" the ego already has its response at the ready. "We must learn to appreciate love by not experiencing it." Really?

Now if you stood back and really examined this statement with the utmost clarity, you might conclude that the ego is out of its proverbial mind. How does one appreciate that which is not experienced? But hold on a minute! The ego has an answer for that one too. "By not experiencing it, you will want it more and will therefore learn how much it means to you." Sort of like when one's beautiful child dies unexpectedly at a very young age. According to this logic, God did you a favor by taking your child away so that you would know how to really appreciate that wonderful human being. In other words, lack produces greater appreciation for that which is lacking. But if the thing that you are supposed to appreciate is now gone, how does that lead to a greater appreciation for it? In reality, it leads to grief, pain, despair, and remorse—not to mention guilt. These are not happy feelings. Yet those who believe the ego's ramblings will try to fit this square peg in a round hole by telling themselves that it is necessary to come to terms with this and find peace anyway. They will often say things like, "The child is better off in heaven anyway." Well, if the child is better off wherever he or she went, then what does that say about life on this planet?

If we were to spiral deeper and deeper into this logic, we would find that it leads to deeper and deeper confusion. The confusion would eventually become impossible to process on a conscious level, and we would therefore repress the experience and attempt to move on to other things.

Why is the ego's logic so confusing? Why can't this just be simple? The answer lies in the ego's fundamental context, which does not question the existence of pain, death, and suffering in the first place. And why do you suppose it would not be an obvious first step to question the existence of such things? Because the ego needs conflict in order to survive.

The heart, on the other hand, has no ambiguity whatsoever. Pain, suffering, and death are just plain wrong. They don't belong. Period.

It is important to understand that this is not a moral issue for the heart. The heart does not know anything about morals. Where are morals needed in a context of Infinite Love? Once again, morals are only valid where love appears *not* to exist in certain places. The subject of morals refers to where one chooses to position themselves in the context of the battle.

The heart is already connected to what we shall refer to as the Real World. The Real World is that of Infinite Love, and nothing else. Do you think that there is no creation in that world? There is more creation than you could ever imagine!

Let us examine another popular, New Age contextual theory about what is going on upon this planet and in the Universe at large. Many people believe that this entire setup of duality is due to the fact that God wanted to split itself off, in order to have other experiences and to therefore know itself better. Dearest friends, God cannot be split like some sort of pie. Think of yourself as a holistic being for a moment. Would it ever occur to you to cut off your hand, leave it somewhere, and walk away so that your hand could know what it was like to be separated from you, and perhaps find its way back to you? And that somehow through this act, you would come to know more about yourself? Would you concede that such an idea, when applied to yourself, sounds a bit insane? And let's not forget that this perception would also include the idea that your hand would learn a valuable lesson in appreciation of how much better it is to be attached to your body!

None of what is being described here has anything to do with creation. Yet in the world that we live in on planet Earth, all creation appears to be generated by division. Even our physical cells are created by dividing. A country is created by dividing itself from all other countries and masses of land. Our identities are created to the extent that we recognize ourselves as separate from others. This can manifest as a group identity or that of an individual. Words are assigned to things in order to differentiate them from other things. Everything is separate. It's no wonder that we turn to equally separated theories to explain God and the Universe to ourselves. To us, it can make perfect sense that God is into separation and division because that is all that we know.

The ultimate separation manifests as the battle between good and evil. The ultimate separation exists in an experience of not knowing God.

But what if we are collectively wrong about all of this? What if that is the real reason that nothing appears to change at the macro level of our collective experience? What if our context is completely erroneous?

The challenge that we propose here is simple. We challenge you, if you are so interested, to challenge the suppositions of the ego, when it comes to planetary evolution on our beloved Earth. We wholeheartedly suggest that you try something else instead. We suggest that for once you listen to the experiential counsel of the heart.

The heart is clear and unambiguous. It pulls no punches in terms of its directly stated position. Some might say that it is difficult to even know what the heart is, much less attune to its messages. It's not that the heart is not clear. It's that we try to filter its messages through the state of duality inherent in the ego. Why would we collectively do this? Because the ego makes a lot more noise. The ego speaks to us in our heads all day long. It judges and evaluates literally every single thing that we come across in our daily experiences. It unceasingly evaluates the past, present, and future. If we are lucky enough to keep it quiet at night, we might get some sleep. But for the most part, the ego is talking to us all the time.

Have you ever noticed the look of clarity and oneness in the eyes of a newborn or very young baby? At what point does this amazing look begin to fade? Quite simply, it begins to fade at the point when the child begins to learn words. Words exist as the language of the ego. We are not suggesting that everyone stop speaking. We are simply demonstrating the place from which the ego derives its voice. Words are never the things that they describe. They exist as labels used to identify one thing as separate from another. In a divided reality such as this one, it would make no sense to eliminate words. It is the perfect language for the ego and for all things separated.

So the ego makes a lot of noise and speaks to us in very authoritative ways. This endless chatter buries the ever-present state of oneness that resides in and emanates from our hearts. The heart has answers. The ego has questions. The duality of the ego causes us to doubt that the heart knows anything, and for some, that doubt extends to questioning the very existence of the heart itself. The ego speaks of its dual state of reality every time it says things like "But" or "Yeah, but what about this?" Its ultimate "yeah, but" moments always include the existence of something horrible or negative.

Let us examine what it might look like if we listen only to our hearts for answers and a new context. The first thing you should know is that the heart is not a predictor of the future. Nor is it a guru, here to tell you what to do. It is not a judge. It does not analyze or evaluate. Those are all mathematical functions of the conscious mind. The heart, quite simply, broadcasts what is true and real every single second. Not what is true and real in a dual state of conflicted reality. The heart will only tell you what is true and real in Infinite Love. To the heart, there is no either/or. There is only the Oneness of Love.

Because we filter everything through the divided ego, and tend to consider it our major authority, we can actually come to believe that the heart has no message at all! To the ego, a state of Oneness in the Universe makes no sense. Everything must be interpreted through a divided state. Every question must have an answer of either/or. The ego looks at the heart and says there's nothing there.

Why don't we take a moment to listen only to the ever-present message emanating from our hearts? Why don't we see what that message feels like without filtering it through the divided ego? Ask the ego, or your conscious thinking mind, to take a break for a moment. Tell it to move aside because you need to pay attention to your heart. You do have the authority to do this. After all, who is in command here?

Now look to see what the heart's position is on death. Does the heart recognize it as a necessary and valid experience? Or does the heart broadcast a world where death does not exist?

What is the heart's position on aging? Does the heart broadcast that God/Love creates deterioration, breakdown, disease, and decrepit states of existence? Does the heart suggest that Alzheimer's is a gift from God? And if that were the case, wouldn't it be an insult to God to try to cure it? On the contrary, the heart will likely broadcast its direct knowledge of a Universe where all life is ageless, vital, and forever alive.

And what do you think the heart's position on relationships might be? Well, that's an easy one. All is simply Love. There is no division. Does the heart tell you of a world where people suffer in their relationships, or in the lack thereof? Does it tell you of a world where people do grave harm to one another in anger and disdain? Does it suggest a world of unrequited love, loneliness, and irreconcilable differences? Of course not. The heart broadcasts a Universe of unity, love, and everlasting fulfillment. It tells you about happiness.

Now before we go on, it should be made clear that the heart should never be confused with emotion. Emotion exists as the chemical reaction to all the different states of duality that exist here. Emotion, as it is experienced on Earth, is the direct result of confusion in the body's chemistry, as the thinking mind projects all manner of conflicting interpretations about what is going on around you and inside of you. The body's chemistry reacts accordingly, which is why emotions can be experienced as such a rollercoaster ride. The ego and the thinking mind can never get their questions and answers straight. It is all conflict, all the time. The mind will tell you that it is your job to resolve the conflicts. This message immediately affects the physical body and produces stress, confusion, and emotional turmoil of varying degrees. In that system, the only way to gain emotional stability is to exert some form of control over oneself, such as what people do when they engage in positive thinking. But if one must engage in positive thinking, it goes without saying that negative thinking is always on your heels. Thus the duality continues to reign.

And let us talk about abundance and prosperity. If you pay attention, you will note that the heart speaks of a Universe where lack is an unknown. It simply doesn't exist. All is provided for in an unlimited way, and peace and harmony are the natural result. Unbridled creation of Love and Infinity are the only things that exist.

It is important to recognize that the ego will automatically invalidate all of the above. Remember that the ego survives only where there is conflict and duality. It literally garners its life force from the friction of these opposing forces. The best way to describe this is that this is what the ego finds exciting. This is the environment in which the ego thrives. The ego will tell you that the main purpose of life is conflict resolution. It will tell you that this is the path to infinity. The only problem, of course, is that the ego will never address the conditions that produce the conflict in the first place. And that is the secret to this entire situation.

CHAPTER 2

From Where Does the Heart Derive Its Knowledge?

Some may think that the heart derives its knowledge from an emotional state or from a state of wishing or hoping. This would not be accurate. The heart exists in "at-one-ment" with what we shall refer to as the Real World. The Real World is that of Infinite, Omnipresent Love.

When you connect the letters in "at-one-ment," it spells atonement. One definition for atonement is agreement or reconciliation. *Atone* means to bring into agreement or to reconcile. *Reconcile* means to make consistent or to bring into harmony. So the heart is therefore consistent with Omnipresent Love. It exists in a harmonious state with that reality. In fact, it *is* that reality.

Let us look very clearly at the exact meaning of "at-one-ment" when it comes to the heart. It means that the heart *is* Omnipresence. The heart *is* God. The heart literally *exists* in the Real World. So what does this mean to you? In order to answer that question, we must first examine the current, erroneous perspective that we collectively tend to have here on Earth. This is important in order to understand the filters that we are perceiving life through.

The first error in perception is that we unwittingly try to locate God, Omnipresence, and the heart in the same space-time continuum as that of this finite reality. We automatically look for such things in terms of what we think should be their linear positions. This is how our five physical senses are geared, and we falsely assume that everything can be known in this way. We look for God in the same way that we might look for a set of lost keys. "Where is it?" we say to ourselves. It is interesting that we assume that God is not anywhere where we are, and we tend to look up into space to locate it there.

In terms of the heart, we know experientially that it is located somewhere in our chest because that is where we tend to feel the center of ourselves when it comes to love. We also know that we have a physical heart, which appears to be located in the same general area. Because we perceive ourselves as primarily physical (and for some it is only physical), anything that cannot be measured in time and space as we know it is difficult to deal with because we have no way to physically prove to ourselves that it exists. This point is vitally important to understand because it is the reason that we tend to doubt the things that are most necessary for us to know.

The first thing to accept is that God cannot be physically located in the finite, physical world. That does not mean that you will not see manifestations of divinity. It means that the finite, physical world asks us to see everything according to its own terms of existence. If something cannot be recognized in those terms, then its existence and its validity will automatically be in question.

So what are the terms of the finite, physical world? Quite simply, everything here is known by what it is *not*. For example, you know you are poor only because you are not rich. Likewise, you know that you are rich only because you are not poor. You know that you are a woman because you are not a man. You know you are a man because you are not a woman. You know that you are a child because you are not an adult and vice-versa. We know everything through a filter of contrast.

Happiness can be identified because it is not sadness. And likewise, sadness can be known as that which is not happy. Now here is a very key and critical point. If everything in this finite, physical world is known through a filter of contrast, and we mean *everything*, what does this say about knowing God? What does this say about knowing Love?

According to these terms of knowing through this finite existence, God can only be known by what it is *not*. Love can only be known by virtue of the existence of hate. Otherwise, we have no way to recognize it in this physical world. And this clearly explains our collective addiction to pain, suffering, and death. According to the terms of the finite, these things are necessary in order for us to be able to recognize love, harmony, and everlasting life. We have made pain, suffering, and death into a spiritual religion because here in the finite, it is deemed the only way to appreciate and know God. According to the laws of the finite, God does not exist without this contrast.

There are certain conditions present in the finite that produce this primary filter of contrast as the only clear way in which to know anything. The problem on this planet is that we tend to stop our knowingness at these primary filters. In fact, we don't even realize that such filters exist. We tend to believe that this is it. There is nothing more, so we perceive.

What if these filters are simply not valid in the wider Universe of all creation? What if knowing through contrast is peculiar to our situation here? This notion exists as a profound and powerful paradigm shift in perception. We are finally in a place on an evolutionary basis where we can begin to stand back from this filter and actually see it for what it is rather than only seeing *through* it. The process that this involves is as simple as taking off a pair of glasses that you didn't know you were wearing. But what is different about these glasses is that instead of acting as an aid to knowing, they actually make you blind to most of what you need to recognize and see.

The heart does not wear such glasses. The heart possesses no filters. It is pure, unadulterated Love. It is pure, unadulterated God. This is why it is so difficult to recognize. There is no contrast in the Real World of the heart.

So let us remove the filters of the finite in order to fully know what the heart is telling us and to fully recognize what the heart eternally broadcasts and radiates about the Truth. If this seems daunting, consider this. Your everyday perception consists of the following: What will seem the most real to you on planet Earth is everything that is filtered through contrast. Behind this veil shines the ever-present heart. But because this veil of contrast lies in front of it, what is powerfully broadcast from the heart in the full, infinite, radiating power of divine Love will seem more like a whisper, or perhaps not be seen or felt at all. The mind, whose job it is to interpret everything through this exact same veil, will try to help you out by informing you that the heart's signal is weak, inconsequential, or simply nonexistent. It will tell you that relying upon it is risky business at best. It will tell you that the heart is vague and not to be trusted. Remember, in a world where everything is known by what it *isn't*, anything known only by what it *is* cannot be trusted as valid. There is simply no basis for it in our outside world of perception.

The heart is infinite presence. The filter of contrast produces an illusion that all things are finite. Therefore, we know God by what it is *not*. We therefore say that God is *not* here. God takes on the same vagueness or diminutiveness as our experience of the heart. Thus we cannot readily see or feel the presence of God. We attempt to know God through this same filter, and find contrast and contradiction everywhere we look.

Think for a moment about the biblical story of Genesis and the Garden of Eden. This is a perfect metaphor for what we have just described. The serpent tempts Eve and then Adam to eat from the tree of the knowledge of good and evil. Need we say more?

The knowledge of good and evil clearly refers to this filter of contrast. This one simple concept is the source of all confusion, delusion, and illusion. How can there possibly be good *and* evil, after all? The truth is that there can't be. It is all an illusion caused by one singular source. The exact makeup of that source and its matrix is explained in *The Final Elimination of the Source of Fear*.

Now this is not to say that there is not a clear manifestation of this illusion. Of course there is. We live it every single day on this planetary sphere as we witness and experience pain, death, and suffering. Have you ever noticed how often nations look to war to achieve peace? This is another perfect example of knowing something by what it isn't. It is a very strange, yet understandable, knee-jerk reaction to want peace and then use war as a means to achieve it. If peace is known by what it isn't, then more wars would be the best way to get there. In other words, more of what *isn't* peace should make peace more obvious, right?

So on an international scale, countries may want to achieve peace in a certain region. They will attempt to create it in one of two ways, but always by using the laws of contrast. The first way is to create war. In other words, it is like saying, "We will create so much war in your country that you will be begging for peace!" Remember the idea that the way to appreciate something is by its absence? This is the means by which one military defeats another psychologically. The second way is to hold the contrasting idea of "no war" and to promote peace as something defined as the *absence* of war. In other words, we know peace because it is *not* war.

As this brand of logic permeates international relations between countries, it is no wonder that confusion and irreconcilable differences continue to reign. How often is "peace" maintained by the threat of war? Is this really peace?

Peace cannot be known by what it is *not*. Yet we accept this illusion every single day, and we consider it real. But our hearts know differently. And therein lies the discomfort.

Have you ever wondered why we are so disconnected from the rest of our Universe? It seems odd, does it not, that we could be this unconscious about something so vast, so huge that surrounds us every day. Granted, we have managed to create technologies that permit us to see into the cosmos and recognize all sorts of interstellar phenomena. But for the most part, such observances are limited to the realm of scientists and their research. In our everyday lives, we are lucky if we remember that Earth revolves around the sun. We still continue to frame that occurrence as "the sun rises and sets," which it doesn't.

Once again, we unwittingly know the Earth by what it is not. It is *not* the entire rest of the Universe. This exceedingly limited experience feels comfortable to us. We are provided with a primitive sense of security because we tend to perceive our planetary realm as the only life there is. We live as though there is nothing else. Our attempts to "conquer" space through our technologies do not in any way impinge upon our illusion that we reside at the center of all that is. We are simply stretching out to take over other worlds and bring them into the fold of how we see the Universe.

How does this filter of contrast affect people in their individual lives? There are countless examples. Have you ever wondered why the more you may try to get rich, the poorer you may experience yourself to be? On a subconscious level, more poverty supposedly means greater appreciation for wealth, which is supposed to translate into more desire. More desire for wealth is supposed to translate into a greater effort to get rich. But it doesn't work because you are stuck in a filter that falsifies the definition of wealth. The filter says that wealth, like everything else, is defined by what it isn't. In other words, wealth is defined by the existence of poverty. So this filter tries to achieve wealth by outlining it with greater poverty—and greater contrast. You, unfortunately, become the mechanism of poverty designed to amplify the perception of wealth. On some deep, unconscious level, the belief is that if you can amplify this perception of wealth by being poor, then such wealth will become more evident, and therefore closer to your grasp.

Another common example of this same manifestation is found in the scenario where a person is desperate to find a loving relationship. The harder they try, the worse things get. They may even find people virtually fleeing from them without explanation. In their desperation, they will begin to make statements like, "There are no good men or women left" or "I am destined to be alone for life." How can this help? This particular filter is causing them to emphasize their loneliness more and more, in an effort to produce contrast with the idea of a beautiful, loving relationship, thereby making it more visible and thus more accessible. This is precisely why you will see people doubling down on their negative statements when they are unable to create what they really want.

The two scenarios described above show exactly how the filters of contrast can amplify the conditions of what you do not want. Your effort to be rich can produce greater poverty. Your effort to find a loving relationship can produce greater aloneness and loneliness. If you can understand this, you will begin to see what a roundabout, futile way this is to produce anything. It will always and inevitably produce only the opposite of what you say you want.

The heart is a fascinating alternative. The heart is solely about pure creation. Pure manifestation. From where does it derive this knowledge?

The heart *is* the Real World. In the Real World, there is no duality. Everything is known by what it *is*, remember? Contrast is not necessary. Things are appreciated and loved by experiencing them. Life does not have to be extinguished in order to be recognized as something that you want. Therefore, life is eternal. There is no need for death to provide a contrast. Beauty is known in its pure state as beauty. It does not require ugliness in order to be recognized. Are you starting to get the idea? If you want to create something, you simply create it. There is no such thing as creating contrast and opposites in order to see and then get what you want. That is false, unsustainable creation. And it *is* unsustainable.

What do you think change is all about? These ever-present forces of conflict and contrast produce a volatile soup of instability, and whatever we create must be constantly maintained and forcibly held together to prevent it from falling apart. We exercise to prevent atrophy. We have to keep practicing any skill in order to keep it strong. What happens if you don't maintain vigilance in supporting friendships and relationships? They begin to deteriorate. Why does positive thinking require a never-ending effort? Does this seem natural to you? It doesn't to the heart.

The heart doesn't believe in any of this because the heart already lives in the world where such things are absolutely unnecessary. It really does live there right now! This is not a future happening. This is where eternity lives. What does this mean to you in your everyday life? It means that you already live in eternity. You already exist in a Universe where the filters of conflict and contrast do not exist. The amazing thing is that this world is far more real than the one you think you live in where struggle, pain, and suffering rule the day—where one must exert considerable effort to find any moments of solace and peace. Where one must grieve over death and dying in order to appreciate life.

The mind will tell you that a world of Love, Peace, and Eternity is boring. It will tell you that there is nothing to do. Nothing to achieve. But you must take into consideration the mind's paradigm. It is the designated filter for reality. It does a perfect job of this; it invalidates anything that does not fit into its paradigm of contrast and conflict. So it perfectly weaves a perspective of illusionary contrast for you as it acts as an overlay to the Real World of the heart.

Now let us put to rest once and for all the mind's claim that there is nothing to do or achieve in the Real World of Infinite Love. How about *unlimited* creation of anything and everything that exists as a manifestation of Love? We don't know about such things here because we are like the proverbial car stuck in the ditch, spinning our wheels and dying before we get anything done. We endlessly repeat the same things over and over again, in different forms, as we tell ourselves that this is a wonderful path that is getting us somewhere. But where is this "somewhere" that we think we are getting to? In truth, it doesn't exist. Have you noticed that yet?

But do not worry because the mind has an answer for that too. "It will happen after you die!" claims the mind. We look toward death to provide some relief for our frustration. "Surely things are better on the other side," we tell ourselves. Well, if they are better, then what are we doing here?

It should be said at this point that the mind will not like this line of conversation. Without death as an escape hatch, the mind becomes very insecure. It is important to have that invisible "other side" as a way to increase our tolerance of these contrasting filters. It acts like a pressure-relief valve in our consciousness. It lulls us into complacency while we falsely await salvation as our "reward" for leaving the planet.

Although the mind may feel insecure, there is absolutely no reason for *us* to feel insecure. Remember that the mind is only a filter. It is a processing machine. It processes reality for us and acts as a false interpreter. How do you know it is false? Because it includes all manner of conflict, confusion, and irreconcilable uncertainties. How can this be real? The truth is that it can't be. The mind is a filter, not the truth.

Your heart, on the other hand, is absolutely trustworthy. You will never see conflict there. There is only Oneness, Infinity, and Love. Which would you rather rely upon for the truth in your perception?

CHAPTER 3

What about Fear?

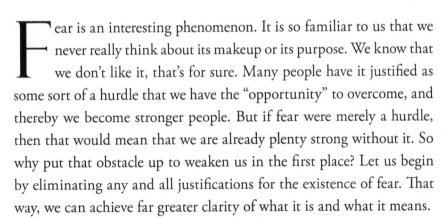

Fear is an interesting phenomenon. It is so familiar to us that we never really think about its makeup or its purpose. We know that we don't like it, that's for sure. Many people have it justified as some sort of a hurdle that we have the "opportunity" to overcome, and thereby we become stronger people. But if fear were merely a hurdle, then that would mean that we are already plenty strong without it. So why put that obstacle up to weaken us in the first place? Let us begin by eliminating any and all justifications for the existence of fear. That way, we can achieve far greater clarity of what it is and what it means.

Fear exists as an integral part of our finite existence. Finite means that we have a beginning and an end in terms of how we identify ourselves here. Fear exists as a part of that matrix. Then what is the purpose of fear? In order to answer that question, let us look at what happens when one is afraid.

The first thing that happens is withdrawal. Simultaneous to the withdrawal is resistance. So you have withdrawal and resistance. Withdrawal and resistance are instantaneous reactions to something. Fundamentally, they are reactions to any threat to one's finite identity. Whatever it is that you identify as having anything to do with who you perceive yourself to be can potentially be threatened by something else. The most obvious example of this would be related to your physical body. If you feel physically threatened, you will definitely experience fear.

Your perception of self can also be threatened mentally and emotionally. If they are *your* thoughts and *your* emotions, they certainly can be threatened by something else. This is generally the source of most conflict in relationships. For example, if you hold certain beliefs and feelings about money, and you experience those to be a definite part of your own psychology and identity, a partner with opposing views can be threatening if you feel obliged to take on his or her perspective. Why? Because they are asking you to change some part of your own psychology and alter your identity in some way. There are countless examples of this, and money is only one of them.

So this example of financial conflict is ultimately not about money at all. If it were only about money, both parties could easily externalize it without a threat to either one. Both people could come to some simple, reasonable conclusions *together* about what might be the best path to follow in order to obtain mutually beneficial results. But this conflict is really about identity, and money is merely the subject of the conversation.

The potential threat to one's identity can also extend beyond the physical body. It can include possessions. This explains why people will oftentimes put themselves in grave physical danger by staying in their homes when an out-of-control wildfire is on its way or an extreme hurricane is about to occur. In their experience, the threat to their homes is as grave as if it were a direct threat to their own physical existence.

If relationships and friendships form an integral part of a person's identity, then fear and jealousy can overtake those relationships. Serious control issues can manifest. And yet, these issues are never really about the other person. Such issues can arise when one person is unable to distinguish between perception about another person and the reality of that individual. If perception of another person is incorporated into one's own identity, then that other person's behavior becomes threatening if it conflicts with that perception.

A particular group can be integrated into one's consciousness as a part of a person's identity. This is how cults are formed. Try prying someone away from a cult, and you will find out how much that person believes that he or she and the cult are one and the same.

A city or country where one lives can also be construed as a major part of who a person believes he or she is. Religions, clubs, schools, activities, and lifestyles can perform the same function. There is simply no end to all of the ways and means by which people form identities of who they think they are. And every single one of these ways exists as a potential to feel threatened, and thus afraid, if there is any sense that it could be changed or taken away.

This need to preserve one's finite identity can even supersede your best intentions to change in a positive way. For example, on a physical level, if a person wants to lose weight and has been what they consider overweight for many years, it is likely that their current physical size has been fully incorporated into his or her identity. It can be extremely difficult for that person to visualize themselves at a smaller size. Subconsciously, the loss of weight will be perceived as an identity threat and will therefore be resisted, even if that excess weight is making that person miserable.

This threat to identity is a common occurrence when it comes to healing a long-term injury or health condition. It is likely that after a certain period of time, the illness or injury will be incorporated as "*my* illness" or "*my* injury." To the subconscious mind, it is no different than any other part of one's identified embodiment, even if it is totally unpleasant. So rather than the body comprehending healing, the body may instead see the malady as an issue to hold on to in order to preserve the person's overall identity.

If we are creators, then why would there be something that is perceived as a threat to one's identity? That fascinating question can only be answered by understanding the function of fear. Fear's main function is to preserve all aspects of one's identity in a finite reality. It's that simple. The very nature of this finite Universe makes fear an essential component of life.

So let us discuss what this means in terms of being a lightworker. Before you ever thought of yourself as a lightworker, you probably had fashioned a well-established identity for yourself. Whether you perceived that identity as good or bad was not important. What was important was the prime directive that existed in your finite intelligence to preserve that identity. This is not necessarily something that you could have done anything about since this need to preserve is as innate as your DNA.

So something likely happened that moved you into a new understanding that perhaps you had a higher purpose. The struggle to align with a higher purpose is for the most part a struggle with identity. A higher purpose could be as simple as becoming a better, happier person so as to exert a more positive influence on those around you. It could be as profound as a complete and total change in career, lifestyle, and relationships. Or it could be anything in between. It could include a massive spiritual overhaul in terms of how you see yourself in the Universe. Or it could be as simple as a desire to reconnect with and do something in support of nature. The possibilities are as unique and unlimited as each individual human being. But wherever these possibilities include a change in perspective, activity, or otherwise, you will likely feel resistance or outright fear. Let us first say that this is not your fault. There is no point in identifying with the fear because, in truth, you did not create it. In fact, fear is not a creation at all! It exists as *resistance* to creation.

The resistance is not your fault either. You did not create this finite universe that gives rise to a perpetual state of resistance when it comes to God and Omnipresence. Now before you interpret these statements as some accusation of powerlessness, listen further.

This finite universe is an illusion based upon the first, original lie. That lie is quite simple to comprehend. It is the lie called "I am *not* God" or "I am *not* Omnipresence." These statements are not possible, which is how you can easily recognize them as untrue. There is no such reality as "*not* Infinite." Therefore, there is no such reality as finite. It simply doesn't exist, except as an illusion or a dream. If you were to imagine such a lie at its inception, you would understand that this lie could only beget illusion because such a thing is not possible in reality. Do you want to know what this illusion would look like? Look around you. You are living in that illusion right now. The illusion is called the finite Universe, where many things that claim to be "*not* God" are manifesting. Interesting, isn't it?

So this physical world is a fanciful dream in which seers, sages, prophets, and saints have asked us for millenniums to please wake up! But waking up is an evolutionary process. It is not as though there is a giant alarm clock on a cosmic nightstand somewhere waiting to go off.

If you have fallen into the belief that you, personally, have somehow created all of this, then you are still confused about who you really are. Let us just say that direct knowledge of the specific manifestation of how this original lie was conceived of and then instantly begat our current manifestation of a finite universe, is not available to our current restricted state of intellectual, linear knowledge and the language and parameters that accompany it. That is always a blow to the ego and the conscious, thinking mind, which would like to believe that it can know everything there is to know. Unfortunately, there is not a whole lot that can ever be known in a manifestation of "I am *not* God." The ego should be put on notice that it cannot have it both ways.

Why is it important for you to understand that you did not create fear, resistance, and this finite kingdom of false reality? Because there is no way to believe that you did and simultaneously know who you really are. As long as you believe that these are your creations, you can never exist in your own experience as a manifestation of Infinite Love because the Infinite God cannot give rise to such things.

If you believe that you created fear and all of its insidious underpinnings, then you are, to yourself, as much of an illusion as the world around you, and you are still very sound asleep. And the dream will continue.

A simple way to understand this is to realize that right now you are trapped in the matrix of this first, original lie. How do you know that? Because you exist in a finite body in an equally finite world. It is important to address why death does not free one from any of this. It has to do with the nature of the soul. A soul has finite parameters, just as a body does. A soul has a finite identity just as a physical body does. Granted, a soul can indeed exist in another dimension and pass from one physical lifetime to another, but that does not change its direct relationship to the same finite circumstances.

Now when we use the word *trapped*, we do not mean helpless. Of course you are not helpless. If you were, then all would be hopeless, which it isn't. So how do you change? It absolutely starts with perspective. Perspective leads to perception, which then leads to outcome. The first thing to do is to realize that you didn't create this. You couldn't. An illusion is not a creation. An illusion is only a manifestation of a lie. It is your identification with this lie that produces your entrapment in it. The lie is "I am *not* God."

Merely *believing* that one is God is not enough. That is always easy for the mind, and it is what philosophy and religions are made of. Beliefs. This is where the reality of the heart comes into play. The heart is God, and the heart is you. We must go beneath the matrix of fear and the lie of "I am *not*" in order to experience this.

The lie of "I am *not* God" or "I am *not* Infinite Love" sits across the heart like a negative sentry that lets nothing through. This lie does not exist in words or in thought. It is literally a matrix, which is why you cannot talk yourself out of it. It is prior to all language and human, finite thought. In fact, it is literally what gives rise to human, finite thought.

It has been said many times that there are only two emotions: Love and fear. Actually, these are not "emotions." These are *conditions of consciousness* produced either by Truth, which is a condition of Love, or by the first, original lie, which is a condition of fear. It's that simple. Either condition gives rise to many things. The condition of Truth and Love gives rise to all creation and the infinite beauty and magnitude of the Real Universe. The condition of the first, original lie and its resulting fear gives rise to a Universe of illusion, conflict, and many other confusing, negative results.

Fear is quite literally an experience of the absence of God. Since this is not possible, fear is the experience of an illusion. Its manifestations are manyfold, which is clearly evident in life on Earth as we know it. Even though these manifestations are illusionary, we live through these experiences nonetheless. Fear exists as pure resistance to God and pure resistance to Divine Love. It produces withdrawal from Divine Love and therefore hopelessness. In our hopelessness, we attempt to take control of our lives as separate entities who perceive themselves as abandoned by God. We pray for help in coping with our perceived abandonment, and we hope that someone is listening. So all of our prayers stem from our own illusion.

It should be stated here that there is no useful value in living in a reality of fear and illusion. There is nothing to be learned, and such learning is not necessary. Illusions, on a cosmic level, provide exactly what they are, which is nothing.

It is time that we stop making excuses for the existence of fear. It is time that we stop lying to ourselves and making up stories about why this finite existence of pain, death, and suffering are so important to us. There is absolutely no evidence whatsoever that any of this is important. We are just deluding ourselves. What is important about humankind living in conflict with the entire Universe? What is so important about incarnate human beings having no idea who they are and why they are here?

In some ways, it is as though we live in some strange version of a cosmic Stockholm syndrome. The Stockholm syndrome is a psychological condition where a hostage identifies with and sympathizes with his or her captor. Humankind certainly has cultivated a well-developed habit of doing the same with the source of fear and all of its accompanying conditions. We sympathize with the existence of death, suffering, and pain. We erroneously assign a high spiritual value to such things in order to live through the conditions of entropy surrounding them that create constant wear and tear on our souls.

If you find any of this depressing, it only means that you have chosen to identify with all of it. The purpose of this communication is to help you let go of that identification and remember that you are a creator, not a victim. But it is important to remember that you are a creator in the Universe, not just on planet Earth. This point is vital to know because it returns you to your proper context in which to deal with all of this. It puts you back into a state of command, in terms of who you really are as a creative power in the Real Universe.

Creative powers don't die. They don't feel weak and abandoned by God. In fact, they exist as an extension of God. What else could they be? What else could *you* be? Fear has nothing to do with you, except in this dream called planetary, finite Earth. The key word here is finite. Earth cannot truly be finite any more than anything else in the Real World can be. We are experiencing a collective dream of what Earth would look like if such things as "I am *not* God" were real. Isn't that amazing? And you probably thought that the infinite was a dream. In truth, it's the other way around.

CHAPTER 4

Imagination

Imagination is a power and a key to our true selves. In our currently finite state on planet Earth, it is definitely overshadowed by the source of fear. So let us take a moment to look behind the matrix of the finite to see what imagination really has to show us.

Imagination gives us a glimpse into our true power as creators. We can literally conceive of anything because our imagination exists as a window into the mind of God, of which we ourselves are an extension.

What happens when you place the veil of the finite and the filter of contrast over the innate power of imagination? The entire power goes askew because it is diminished and split into a manifestation of what is inherent in that veil or filter. So rather than functioning as a creator in the Universe, you will find yourself functioning as a creator in the finite. You will find your imagination running amok with illusions and conflict since it subscribes wholeheartedly to the source of fear.

How many times have you found yourself imagining all sorts of terrible things that could go wrong in your life? Interestingly, such imaginings are often deemed to be "realistic" and important, whereas imaginings of beautiful, positive things are often invalidated as "daydreams" or unrealistic wanderings.

Overall, imagination carries a connotation of frivolity, which is not helpful when you realize how significant it is to our collective evolution. If we cannot imagine and realistically believe in something other than what we now know, we will continue to remain trapped in this current paradigm of conflict, death, and the substantial limitation of our finite world. What we are looking for now exists in an entirely new dimension of our gift of imagination. That dimension can be found in that which transcends our collective belief in the source of fear. This is where we must go to learn to connect our imagination with our hearts—instead of connecting it with the ego and the thinking mind.

As we have already stated, the heart exists in "at-one-ment" with God, Infinite Love, and the Real World. This must necessarily be experienced and therefore understood as Reality. If we settle for this as a mere philosophical concept, there will be no practical benefit whatsoever. In order to experience the heart as Reality, let us take the time to actually listen to what it is telling us.

Let's begin with an extreme example. Let's say that someone close to you, someone who you love very much, dies unexpectedly. Your immediate reaction will be "No!" This will happen before you have even a moment to think about it. This will be a manifestation of your true self, your heart, completely rejecting this as real or possible. As the realization of yet another death on this planet sinks in, your mind will try to help you by trying to find some good in it as you make every attempt to adjust to the circumstances and survive. Yet in your heart of hearts, you will never be able to understand why this happened or to truly accept it.

The real reason that you will not be able to understand this in your heart is because the heart is connected to the real world where death and loss do not exist. Death is conflict. It conflicts with life. It cannot be a part of life as so many would like to believe. How can that which extinguishes life be construed as a part of that which it extinguishes? Like so many things in the finite world, this makes no sense at all.

Another good example is aging. Who looks in the mirror, sees their aged, graying face, and says, "This is great! Just what I was hoping for!"? Most people probably view this change with confusion and disbelief. Why is that? If aging is natural, then why wouldn't we welcome it? Because the heart can never accept this in a Universe of Reality where all is infinite, vital, and permanently alive. The heart recognizes the content of our finite dreams as bizarre and unreal. The mind, on the other hand, explains it away as just another part of "nature." Well, sure it is, if you want to cite the nature of a finite Universe of conflict and unreality.

And this is where we are presented with a choice to go with the Real World of the heart and its knowledge of our *true* nature as infinite beings of light and divine Love. Or we can continue to choose to believe in the nature of the dream of our finite world. This is a tough choice to make because while we are sound asleep, the primary evidence seems to be that of the dream.

The heart presents us with the nature of a Universe of Infinite Love, Light, Joy, and unlimited creation. The mind and the ego present us with a perfect version of the nature of a finite kingdom of conflict, death, pain, and suffering. These are very different realities, and it is time that we learn to differentiate between them. As long as we continue to pretend that the one that we know in this finite, planetary kingdom is all there is, we shall never be free of the necessity to rationalize it, justify it, and continue to explain it away. All of which is to our detriment since it only solidifies the trap that we find ourselves in. Why? Because there is no hope if we continue to affirm that this is all okay on some remotely spiritual level. There is no hope as long as we continue to purport that we find value in pain and suffering.

We are very used to listening to the mind for all of our information about where we live in the Universe. It is a deeply ingrained, unconscious habit. We are not used to listening to our hearts. It is mandatory that we learn to shift our primary reference point from the mind to the heart if we are ever to evolve out of our situation of what appears to be a permanent state of duality. But it is only as permanent as we deem it to be. As long as we continue to accept this filter of good/bad, right/wrong, life/death, happy/sad, etc. and continue making excuses for it, we shall not be able to wake up from this very old dream.

As far as imagination is concerned, the primary thing to understand is that when it is filtered through the ego and the mind, you get the same duality that you see everywhere else. You will also get the same level of confusion, vagueness, and uncertainty. This is why it is imperative to shift our imaginations back into unity with our hearts. In so doing, the imagination is no longer imaginary. Now it exists as the power of creation.

At this point, it should be emphasized that we are creators. We are not victims. The source of fear and its underlying matrix of reality produce a dream world filled with conflict, where our creatorship is virtually lost as we expend all of our energy (of which there is now a limited amount) on solving conflicts and dealing with obstacles. Does this sound like the world of a creator? Of course not.

Our purpose is to realign you, within yourself, to the Real World of creatorship. It is not a world of duality and limitation. It is not a world of death and pain. Those things do not exist as creations of any kind. They are direct manifestations of the first, original lie.

Take a moment now to focus on your breath, and the center from which your breath originates. You will notice that the center exists precisely where you find your heart. The heart, when clearly experienced, always rests in a state of perfect peace. There is no agitation there. Be careful not to confuse emotional agitation with the heart. They are very different. For one thing, emotions in general are pretty much always agitated in one form or another. This is not a shortcoming on your part. What do you expect them to do when the matrix of their entire reality is one of survival and unresolved conflict?

The agitated emotions are connected to—and are a byproduct of—the dream of duality. The peace of the heart is reality. Make sure that you distinguish between the two. If you don't, you will make the mistake of thinking that your job is to quiet your emotional stream of existence. We are not interested in fixing the dream. We are interested in waking you up.

So what does imagination reveal when it is put back into its proper place within the heart? This is a fascinating question because it asks us to consider the difference between the conflicted, unreal dream visions of the mind, and the openly solid, entirely real manifestations of joy in the Real World of the heart. We have been programmed by this false reality to see this in complete reverse. We believe that the dream vision is real, and that Reality is the dream. We don't just think this; we literally experience it this way! We are walking around in a three-dimensional dream of reflected light, and we would swear that this dream forms the basis for all reality. It doesn't. In fact, it doesn't form the basis for any reality whatsoever. It is all an illusion.

As we said before, imagination is a creative power. When the power of imagination is filtered through the mind, the mind, being a dutiful servant of the finite, will tell you that the purpose of imagination is to imagine ways to fix the dream and make it better. It will tell you to think of ways to change the dream into one of more love. It will present you with a false set of precepts and logic, and then it expects you to incorporate that into your mission. It's not the mind's fault. That's all it knows how to do. The mind, in actuality, is what you get when you filter your divine intelligence through the matrix of fear.

We are now going to present you with an interesting exercise. This exercise is designed to realign and strengthen your creator capabilities.

> *Close your eyes. Follow your breath, and note its origin of movement as the source of your breath emanates from your heart. On a physical level, the movement of your breath will flow up and down through your torso. But the divine source of life resides in your heart. As your breath flows up and down, in and out, find your center of rest in the unwavering peace that is your heart. Let yourself magnetically connect and rest there. Allow yourself to feel attracted to this place.*

Next we are going to give you an opportunity to reconnect the imagination to the heart instead of the head. There is a distinct difference between the two experiences. The head is the world of dreams; the heart is the world of reality.

> *Stay at rest within your heart. Open your consciousness to a desire for life that you have within you. It will instantly appear. It might be something that you have wanted for a very long time, but you gave up on it because the mind had presented you with all kinds of conditions that you could not fulfill. Now you are going to see what imagination looks like when centered in the heart, where there are no conditions on creation because all is love. The beauty of this is that there will be no fear or apprehension because you are no longer perceiving through the filter of the dream. You are no longer perceiving through conflict.*
>
> *As you enter this space, you will notice fragments of old perceptions related to this desire, asking you to incorporate the same limitations as before. These fragments will be*

instantly shattered by the heart's energy because they are unsustainable in the Real World. You will watch what happens in a world where such conflicting notions cannot exist.

With every fragment of doubt and limitation that shatters, the experience of your desire will become more and more real. Because this desire is now connected to your heart, instead of your mind, it will become so real that it will begin to feel like it is actually occurring.

At this point, it is important to notice where this reality is being produced. You will note that it is not happening in your head. It is literally manifesting from your heart, with a power that you have never before experienced in the dream. This will affect you profoundly, as you recognize that you have literally awakened to a world of substance and possibility that could never be possible in a finite dream of conflict and limitation.

No one has to tell you that this is real; you will recognize it to be so.

At first, when you engage in this exercise, it may feel as though you are stretching through a formerly tight envelope of consciousness. We urge you to press through it and watch as that envelope starts to disintegrate and finally begins to disappear.

When you feel that you have sufficiently indulged in your creative presence for this session, you will notice that doing this only once profoundly changes the perception of your everyday world. Your physical world will become more real to you, and more tangible. Your senses will be heightened and imbued with greater clarity.

This exercise will have a profound effect on your everyday reality because perhaps for the first time ever, you have activated and engaged your real power as a creator.

Some very odd things may begin to happen after this. You will notice that in engaging with your desire in this way, you will come away fulfilled—again, as though it really happened. It will feel like magic! You will experience an immediate sense of empowerment in your life. It will be as though you have awakened the infinite within. And you have!

We encourage you to do this exercise as often as you are able to. At least once a day is a good idea. You will come to welcome it and look forward to it because you will begin to find yourself in this exercise.

Let us now discuss exactly what is happening here. In this exercise, you are shifting your imagination back to where it belongs, in the domain of the heart. This is where there are no filters, so you are experiencing unbridled creative energy. The same energy with which universes are created. One can no longer effectively refer to this as imagination. In the heart's domain, you are quite literally dealing with the vision of God. You have become one with that vision, as it personally pertains to you.

As long as you harbor an out-of-alignment distortion, produced by the matrix of the finite, where this same visioning power of God is being filtered through the finite, conflicted mind, you will be left with something that is not really manifesting. It is, as the definition goes, imaginary. So even though you may be imagining scenes of true, heartfelt desire, those scenes will be fraught with conflict, limitation, and numerous "what ifs." You will have absolutely no experience that such things have actually manifested because they remain in the unreal realm of highly conditional possibilities. They can easily remain in the realm of wishful thinking.

There is another easy way to tell the difference between unbridled creative power that sits in alignment with the heart and the filtered visioning that sits in the mind. If it sits in the mind, you will know it because you will see it there. It is often referred to as "the mind's eye." There is nothing wrong with this, as long as this is all that you want. But how much good has it done you overall? It provides a great escape, to be sure. But is escape what you're really looking for? Or do you want to get your *self* back?

When this power to imagine sits in the domain of the heart, you will know that as well. You will be experiencing this visioning *from* your heart. That experience will begin to radiate through your entire body and your entire being as physically and dimensionally real. You will have allowed yourself to enter the Real World of things. The power will only grow because there are no filters of limitation. There is no fear. This is the beginning of what life can be like with no filters.

There is one more thing to notice about the difference between imagination residing in the head and the exact same power unfiltered in the heart. If you engage in filtered, head-centered imagination, it will actually take you away from the everyday consciousness about your life. That's why it's called daydreaming. When you snap out of it, you realize that you have missed time, and that this experience has had no effect whatsoever on your physical, everyday life, other than to produce distraction and cause you to be late for things that perhaps you should have been attending to. It is extremely difficult to release this creative energy into manifestation, as it is completely bound in the filters of the finite. Those who manage to do so will testify that it takes a tremendous amount of focus, will, and consistency of effort. Don't you think that putting pictures and notes all over your walls to remind you of what you want is testimony that something is very wrong here, if this is what it takes?

Imagination that originates directly from the heart and is unfiltered by the finite world of conditions and limitations is the unbridled, creative power of God. It can be as gentle as a tiny flower or as powerful as an entire galaxy. When you engage from here, as in the exercise we described earlier, whatever manifests is real. The only manifestation that comes from this place is that of Love. Therefore there is no conflict. The amazing thing about this experience is that it does not take you away from your everyday life. In fact, it will influence it greatly in completely positive ways. It will increase your focus, your power, and your energy. It will make your everyday life more *real* in a wonderful way. It will increase your level of clarity. Even a tiny drop of this experience will be wholly transformational!

Please give yourself permission to make this change. The mind will likely argue with you, as it won't want to lose its position in your currently out-of-alignment state. It will tell you all kinds of things to dissuade you, so allow us to give you a preview of its most common argument. It will simply tell you that this will never work for you. Sound familiar? And the whole time you are trying, it will try to horn in on your effort by informing you about whether or not it's working. It will do this in the form of a question that sounds something like the following: "Is it working? Is it working?"

The agitation that the mind will express is not really about whether or not it's working. (It can't *not* work. It's who you are, for heaven's sake!) The mind's agitation is really about the fact that it doesn't know what to do with a reality where there is no conflict. So it will try to take your simple effort and introduce conflict into that effort by asking if it's *really* working. This is basically an irrelevant question to the situation at hand because you are no longer operating in a dimension of doubt, limitation, fear, and conflict. Recognize that the mind is just trying to do its usual job of filtering through conflict and contrast by attempting to contrast *you* with this simple exercise by saying it doesn't work. So go ahead and expect this highly predictable reaction from the mind. It really is of no consequence if you understand what is going on.

CHAPTER 5

Inspiration

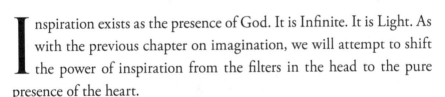

Inspiration exists as the presence of God. It is Infinite. It is Light. As with the previous chapter on imagination, we will attempt to shift the power of inspiration from the filters in the head to the pure presence of the heart.

Inspiration and imagination are intimately tied to one another. That is why it makes no sense to leave inspiration in the domain of the mind, after having shifted imagination into the realm of the heart. These two things exist as the faculties of a creator, and it is imperative that they are experienced with the pure clarity of the heart rather than by filtering them through the distortions of a conflicted mind.

Intuition leads us to inspiration. It could be said that intuition is the fragrance of inspiration that leads us to the flower. Intuition is defined as the ability to know something directly without conscious reasoning. Thus, it doesn't exist in the dimension of the mind, which is why it is so often dismissed when the mind is running the show. According to the mind, which exists as a filter in service to the finite and the source of fear, if something cannot be processed in a linear, finite way, then it is to be deemed irrelevant.

It should be noted here that it is entirely unnecessary to try to fight the mind. The conscious, thinking mind simply has no other way to function. It is a necessary component of living in the finite; without it, you would not even find your way home from work. So let it do what it does best, but you don't have to let it run the show. You, as a creator, should be in command. Not the filtering mind. Think of the mind as an interpreting device whose function should probably be limited to interpreting the logistics of our finite world. It should not be used as a spiritual advisor, a relationship advisor, or otherwise. This is most certainly just asking for trouble and confusion.

The problem is that we are used to asking the mind's advice about everything. *What do I think about such and such?* As we try to figure out what we think about things, the mind (which is already in over its head) can never decide what the right answer is. This problem occurs because it must always weigh its own version of the pros and cons of any situation. No surprise, right? No, it's just more of the same duality where everything has two sides. A plus and a minus, a good and a bad, etc.

The only time that the mind is really sure about anything is when it is trying to protect the ego or the false identity. That is a deeply embedded program that is easy for the mind to process. The answer will generally come in the form of a judgment, which is based only on that particular mind's program of identity. This is why all people judge things differently. It depends on their personalized program of assumed identity. Any time that you argue with someone, it is generally only about one issue. Whose identity is going to be compromised by giving in to the other? Kind of silly, isn't it?

In the Real World, there are no such problems because there is no such thing as a false identity, and there is no such thing as an identity that can be threatened. All is a manifestation of Omnipresence, so there is only Oneness. Is God going to argue with itself? Of course not.

The beautiful thing is that we can begin to live in this Real World now. It no longer has to be seen as a future event. Why is that? It is because people are finally giving up. They are finally ready to give up all of the excuses and all of the justifications. In short, many are just fed up with all the explanations for the finite world of fear and conflict, and they have simply had enough. The excuses and explanations are all so very old, and nothing fundamentally changes because of them. So what if someone says that you are in pain because God wanted it that way? This does absolutely nothing to alleviate that pain, which is what your heart knows needs to happen. The heart is not the least bit confused about the situation. As far as the heart is concerned, it's pain begone! Period. There is no other acceptable outcome. The heart does not sit around studying the whys and the wherefores. The heart simply knows that the pain should not exist.

So who is your best friend? The heart, of course. Wouldn't it be wise to begin listening to it? The heart will never suggest that you should ever, ever suffer. As far as the heart is concerned, you should only experience joy. And how about peace and tranquility? What about abundance and love? These are the only intentions that your heart is capable of. It's the finite, thinking mind that presents you with an entire smorgasbord of negative opportunities.

Let us review where we are so far. The heart is our center of the Universe because it exists in "at-one-ment" with God, Divine Love, and Omnipresence. The mind is a processing medium, which exists in service to the finite world. It filters all of our experiences and interprets them into a finite form of conflict and contrast. Fear is the experience of an illusion called the absence of God, which exists as an illusion because such a thing is not possible. Imagination is the creative power of God, which in our world is generally filtered through the mind, instead of being experienced at its origin, which is the heart. And now, we are ready to talk about inspiration, which is the catalyst that fires the imagination.

Inspiration can be described as the presence of God, but also as the will of God. Inspiration is a beautiful experience, always enlivened with love and joy. It can even be thrilling at times. It always has the effect of igniting creativity. If it were not for the filtering mind, which tends to block anything that cannot be translated into duality, we would live in an inspired state nearly all the time. Inspiration is the presence of God, extending immediately into the will of God, and therefore igniting the imagination with new ideas, which then translate into creation. All such creation exists as a manifestation of Love. Ideally, you can see how important inspiration is!

Stop and ponder for a moment how often you tend to feel truly inspired. If those moments are few and far between, it is a sign of how much your mind is running the show. The thinking, conscious mind would rather be in charge, all by itself, as it continually attempts to advise you about what you "think" you should do. Ever heard of writer's block? This is a perfect example of the mind trying to take over for inspiration. The mind will block what should be a never-ending flow of inspiration for the writer, and it will try to insert itself into that stream of consciousness with all of its good ideas.

The only problem is that the mind cannot substitute for that never-ending flow of divinity in action; once it succeeds in getting the writer to insert the mind in place of this flow, it looks around, realizes that it is in totally unknown territory, and simply has nothing to contribute! What the mind really wants to do is to keep the writer in a finite state of duality, where there is no divine flow of creativity. The mind is so used to being in charge of everything else that it figures it should be in charge of the writing too. It attempts to filter whatever assignment the writer is working on, and it has nothing new to say except that which the writer already knows. Creativity comes to a grinding halt, and the work changes into that of the writer trying to *think* of what to say.

If you are a writer experiencing writer's block, it is first important that you understand what is happening. Don't try to fight the mind. It is simply doing the only thing that it is capable of. Realize that you have inadvertently shifted your creative imagination into its old positioning where the mind now gets to filter everything. And most importantly, remember that the mind is incapable of coming up with any new ideas. It can only offer something that is a version of what is already known—or something it has adopted from someone else. It exists as a filtering, translating device. It is not a creative power. If, at the point that you experience such a blockage, you react by trying to push the mind into thinking *harder*, you will have an experience akin to a car spinning its wheels in the mud and getting nowhere. You are asking the mind to do something that it simply cannot do, which is to engender true, creative thought.

Artists of all kinds can experience the same form of blocking by the mind. Anytime that you can't "think" of something creatively, you know that the thinking mind is now in charge and the natural flow of inspiration has either diminished or completely disappeared. So if you are a writer, an artist, or anyone seeking to do something new, expansive, and creative, do not fight the mind if it tries to impede your efforts and act as a substitute creator. Instead, seek out the flow of inspiration. It will be much easier to find if you take your focus off the mind.

So how does the mind fit into the topic of inspiration? In order to answer this question, we have to examine the best possible alignment for the mind in our finite world. The first thing to know is that the mind should never be in charge of anything. The mind should always be positioned as a servant to the heart. When the mind becomes a servant to the ego, trouble and conflict begin. The ego will try to take control through the use of the mind because the ego has no way to operate on its own. It exists as a false identity and an illusion with no power of any kind. Without the use of the mind, it can't exist. There is no ego where there is no thought.

When the mind functions in service to the ego, there is a constant struggle for control. What is the ego struggling against? It wants to take the place of God. It wants to be the prime commander of everything in your life. It wants to advise you, control you, and tell you what to do. It exists as an imposter that wants to masquerade as the real you, which it isn't. This is why you may sometimes feel inadequate. It's because the ego is in charge, and the ego is absolutely, always inadequate in the job of pretending to be you. This is where feelings of personal weakness come from. It's because the ego is a pathetically weak substitute for the real you.

Interestingly, when the mind is positioned in service to the heart, it is quiet. There is no need for the incessant mental chatter that is evidenced with the ego because the heart *is* you, and therefore, there is no struggle. There is nothing to prove and nothing to be in control of because the truth of the heart stands on its own. The mind can rest in tranquility and peace, and it can do its job effortlessly in the background. Its job in this case is to assist the creative flow of inspiration by simply translating that flow into practical, finite terms. An example of this could be with a painter. Let's say that the painter is perfectly aligned with a creative flow of inspiration. The mind is functioning in a perfect, unified groove with that inspiration. The painter is inspired to use the color red, and the mind meshes with that inspiration as it assists by compelling the painter to place red paint on the brush. There is no power struggle. There is no trying to figure anything out. There is a seamless oneness to every action in every moment. This is what the mind looks like when it is in a state of perfect surrender to the real you.

You can use this example of the painter to understand the same principle in virtually any situation. It can exist in the arts, in writing, in science, in communication, and even in an ordinary situation such as in what you choose to wear. Inspiration serves in all situations if it is unimpeded by the ego.

Inspiration is also a key point to understand when contemplating your role as a lightworker. There are many people who want to do something for the planet, but they have no idea what that might look like. This is because the ego is in control and either can't think of anything new, or it feels protective of whatever false identity it has already fashioned for you. It doesn't want you to function outside of its own secure box because that is perceived as a threat to its survival. It will effectively block any flow of natural, heartfelt inspiration and fill that hole with questions and doubts instead. This produces feelings of insecurity and uncertainty, causing you to hesitate or do nothing at all. This can produce enormous frustration if your heart is broadcasting something else entirely.

Intuition and true inspiration will never lead you astray. These are powerful creative faculties that are directly linked to God. When these faculties are engaged, in humility and alignment, Divine Love moves forward into the world. Your true intelligence takes over. We like to refer to this as the innate Intelligence Factor. This is a very different faculty than the thinking mind. It is a whole body phenomenon, and it extends well beyond the physical body. It radiates outward inter-dimensionally, and it has no beginning and no ending point. This is impossible for the thinking mind to understand, as it can only process that which has a beginning and an end. It only knows how to process and calculate the Universe in mathematical terms. All mathematics begins with division and has its source in the first, original lie. Therefore, mathematics is essentially illusionary.

You should treat intuition and inspiration as precious; seek them out wherever you can. They are the faculties of God manifesting through you and as you. To express this in the proper order, look at it this way. The heart is you, and the heart is God. The heart is Omnipresent Love. The heart is also the seat of Omnipresent Intelligence born of Love. From this center, all creation in your life emerges. From this center, God is able to express and move in the world, through your divine presence.

This is a state of humility and alignment where nothing need be proven. Creation flows as the expression of Omnipresent Love.

The faculties of creation emerge first as intuition, which is like the beginning whisper of inspiration that is on its way. It is like the subtle fragrance of a beautiful flower that is beckoning you to come near. You could say that intuition is like the whisper of an angel, gently guiding you in a certain direction, but it never interferes with your freedom to choose.

Intuition, when followed with humility and innocence, will blossom into creative inspiration. Inspiration gives birth to imagination, where the intelligence factor reveals the perfect unfoldment of creation in form. This is where the mind becomes a useful tool in this finite world, as it has the power to reveal what this creation might look like in a mathematical universe of finite manifestations. In this case, the mind rests in perfect surrender to the heart. It acts as a quiet servant rather than as an illegitimate master.

You might notice that the ego is not mentioned in this entire scenario. Curious, don't you think?

CHAPTER 6

Heaven

We think a great deal about heaven while on Earth, whether consciously or subconsciously. Of course everyone has his or her own unique version of what heaven means. But isn't it curious how common such an idea is?

The religions of the world have pretty much decided that heaven is a place where you can go after you die. We do not need to discuss it on that level, as more than enough has already been said. The only problem with this idea is that it does nothing to address life as it is experienced right now on planet Earth. So let us start by examining some common perspectives of heaven, as they exist while we are alive on Earth.

The most famous one, of course, is that heaven is a place where God lives, as an old man with a long, white beard. He lives up in the sky, in the clouds, behind a big fence known as the "pearly gates." The reason for this fence is so that he can keep out those who don't belong there.

So this old man sits up there on a throne (very much like a king) and judges everyone on Earth as to whether or not they are good enough and obedient enough to be allowed in after they die. If they are not good enough, they will be sent underground to a different place called hell, and burn in fire forever with no way out. If they are deemed worthy, on the other hand, then they shall be allowed in. People don't really know what they will do once they get in there, but at least they won't be suffering in hell. There are also a bunch of angels playing harps and sitting on clouds up there.

Many religions act as God's advisors on Earth. They are basically God's middlemen whose job it is to teach you how to comply with God's rules that will get you into heaven when you die. Of course, things get very confusing because not every religion agrees on what the rules are. But that's not usually a problem. The simple solution is to send the nonbelievers to hell a little bit faster by slaughtering them in advance. This way, such religions help God by taking some of the burden of judgment away. After all, it's a given that these people are going to go to hell anyway; why put God through all the fuss?

It's hard to imagine this entire scenario as little more than a strange cartoon. Yet it is understandable that it exists because it has all the markings of the finite. It is a linear and time-oriented scenario. While you are on Earth, it is all about the fact that you are *not* there. Remember the original lie of "I am *not* God"? Well, according to this theory, you are *not* in heaven either. It has the obvious duality of good and bad, right and wrong, worthy and unworthy. It has judgment and control. The ultimate duality, of course, is life and death, and heaven versus hell.

It is easy to see why so many have chosen to believe in this scenario. It perfectly fits with what they are already familiar with in their everyday lives.

There are other scenarios that people believe in about heaven. One example is the belief that heaven is where you go after you die, and you will get to do pretty much anything you want. If you like cookies, you can eat thousands of cookies and never get fat. If you like to lie around and sleep all day, you can do that, too. Whatever decadent thing you can imagine on Earth, you can definitely do in heaven. You can live in a palace, or you can live in a tent. It's all available for you in heaven.

The only problem with this scenario is that it still doesn't explain what we are doing here on Earth. If heaven is so great, then why did we come here in the first place? Why not just go directly to heaven and bypass all of this struggle?

The first error in these sorts of beliefs is that heaven is a finite place that is separate from here. If that is so, then heaven is as illusionary as our life in this finite world right now. And therein lies the connection between our lives on this planetary sphere and what we refer to as the afterlife. They are both equally as finite and equally as separate.

Let us put all that aside as so many primitive wonderings. Perhaps it is time that we stop traveling back and forth between these illusionary worlds, in the form of reincarnation and whatever else you may believe in, and consider moving back into the Real World where death and dying do not exist.

Some people view this idea as Ascension, so let us examine that idea. The idea of Ascension comes from something very real. It has to do with the fact that when a person, consciousness, energy, or whatever you want to call it, incarnates into any dimensional reality, it goes without saying that such consciousness will incorporate that body into his or her energy field, and take it with them wherever they go. This can be done multiple times and is virtually unlimited. Why in the world would you take on a body, only to have it destroyed against your will, leaving you in some sort of a backward evolution, as you try to resolve the situation through reincarnating again and again? It makes no sense at all. But that's what happens in a finite Universe.

So the people who believe in Ascension should not be laughed at. They are trying to do something that is utterly natural and fully expected in the Real World. Why wouldn't they expect to do the same here? It's funny that we like to fancy ourselves as being so "modern" and on the cutting edge of everything. Well, believe it or not, our notions about life here are incredibly primitive and utterly backward. We tend to be so full of ourselves that we don't even consider joining the wider Universe of the Real World of life. In fact, just the mere mention of it here is likely to provoke immediate objection and intense argument. We are so busy questioning everything that doesn't match with what our minds already know that we run ourselves in circles and then wonder why everything stays the same.

Ascension is utterly normal, and when it doesn't happen or can't happen, something is vitally wrong. That something wrong doesn't have anything to do with the individuals who are trying. It has to do with the conditions and physics produced in this finite world, which were initially engendered by the first, original lie. Those conditions do not allow for Ascension as a normal matter of course. They actually prevent it. The problem here is with the *matrix* of this reality, not with those who inhabit it. So you might want to consider giving up the notion that natural ideas such as Ascension must be learned as a matter of personal growth and your soul's evolution. This implies that it is human beings who are falling short, when in truth it is the conditions of our environment that make such a normal thing nearly impossible.

This is what the ego always does to trick you. It loves to say that *you* are the one at fault or that *you* are the thing that is somehow inadequate. This is a handy-dandy way of getting you to blame *yourself* and focus on yourself as the problem. The matrix of any given reality gives rise to whatever is possible in that reality. The ego absolutely requires that the matrix of this planetary realm remains what it is, in order for the ego to survive. The ego cannot exist in the Real World.

Imagine this, for a moment. If the matrix of this finite Universe produces the results that we live through every day, in terms of what is possible and what exists in this Universe, and the ego tells you another lie that it is really *your* fault and that it is really *your* personal state of evolution that stands in your way, you will, in believing that lie, do your utmost to solve the problem by fixing yourself. That way, you will become so preoccupied with this effort that you will completely miss what is causing these conditions in the first place. And the ego can happily continue in its supported mode of existence for many more eons to come.

Another trick that the ego uses is one we have mentioned before. It will use more of its twisted logic to tell you another impossible lie. It will tell you that all of this trouble exists because God wanted it this way. Here is why this lie is so sinister and actually diabolically clever. In believing this lie, you are checkmated without even realizing it. This lie creates a paradigm in your consciousness that gravely affects how you pray.

Firstly, it completely undermines your trust in God and in Love. You will always experience an undercurrent of fear and mistrust in praying to God, or in knowing God, because you cannot help but be aware of the so-called facts that this lie purports. The lie purports that God has no problem with hurting you and maybe even hurting you really badly. It purports that God has no issues with depriving you of all goodness in life, which is evidenced in the lives of so many people who are suffering around the world. After all, if tiny, innocent babies can suffer and die every day, why would you be special? This weighs very heavily on your heart whenever you go to pray, whether you are consciously aware of it or not.

It is very difficult to put yourself on the line with God in this sort of a "spiritual" environment. The lie is that God has created pain and suffering. Trust is nearly impossible, and guilt is always imminent.

But the ego doesn't stop here. It is always one step ahead, to make sure you don't wake up to the *real* facts. In case this lie about God creating pain and suffering fails, the ego has another whopper already lined up. It will say that *you* created all of this. It will say that you just wanted to have this experience. Isn't it amazing how we can believe this?

When was the last time that you experienced extreme pain, whether it was physical, mental, or emotional, and were just overjoyed that you had managed to create it? Did you exclaim with a triumphant "Yes!" the last time that happened? No, most likely you did everything in your power to bring that pain to an end as quickly as was humanly possible.

Now here is the real checkmate in all of these lies. If you believe in any of these purported explanations of the ego, it will absolutely influence how you pray, and what you pray for. It will completely influence your intent. Let's imagine for a moment that you have an injury or some other problem that is causing you pain. Maybe it's an emotional problem or a circumstantial one. But whatever the case, it is causing you enormous distress. You already have a context for this problem, whether you are aware of it or not. Your context will be influenced by whatever you believe is true about life and about God, or the lack of God, if you are an atheist.

Most likely, you have accepted the conditions on this planet as "the way it is." The belief as to what should be done about it will vary from person to person, but overall, the ego has been very effective at getting nearly everyone to believe that somehow God and you (meaning human beings) are the creators of all of this mayhem. So if you pray, you will naturally pray for help with your own individual problem. But the context of your prayer can be in conflict with your request for help. If you believe that God has sanctioned the existence of pain in whatever form, that belief directly conflicts with your personal request to end it. How do you know for sure that God didn't mean for *you* to experience pain right now?

And then you probably have the ego butting into your prayers, and saying, "It's not possible," "You're not worthy," or "This is all your fault, you know." The ego loves to finish by saying, "God doesn't love you," and "Of course you know you can't count on God for anything, so you better just deal with it."

We are by no means suggesting that you stop praying to God for help in your life. To ask for personal help is *always* a wonderful idea! We are simply asking you to consider enlarging your context. We are suggesting that you pay attention to your heart, and consider discarding the ego's insane ideas.

Here is something new to consider. As you continue to pray for your own life, and for this planet and everything on it, and as you continue to do whatever you do for the benefit and betterment of all, are you interested in expanding the context of your prayers and intentions to a level that perhaps you have never considered? If you are able to grasp the idea that there is a very specific matrix that produces the possibility for pain and suffering to exist, and that this matrix is created by an impossible lie called "I am *not* God," how might that change the nature of your prayers and intentions?

Might you therefore ask that such a manifesting lie and its accompanying matrix be permanently eliminated? Do you think that might be better than merely asking for help to cope with the existence of such because you have unwittingly believed that this is all there is and therefore it must be so? Might you have complete and total confidence in making this request and holding this intention because you would realize, by listening to your heart, that this illusion has nothing to do with God and Divine Love, and therefore cannot be real?

And what do you suppose produces this level of confidence and clarity? It is something incredibly simple. You simply have to be genuinely fed up with the excuses, fed up with the explanations for it all, and fed up with the millennia of failed attempts to rectify any of it. Not fed up in an angry sense. No, that would only defeat the purpose and exist as more of the same. It is more along the lines of you're just not buying into any of it anymore. You've had enough. The excuses don't make any sense, and the explanations are downright absurd. If God is Love, it cannot possibly create—much less conceive of—pain, death, sorrow, and suffering. Period. There is no such thing as you *not* being

God, if God is infinite, therefore you can't create any of it either. Perhaps it is time to be done with this illusion and simply move on.

And here is another thing that perhaps should be pointed out, given that this book is signed and partly written by Archangel Michael. Many people have said that Archangel Michael is here to help us with our fears. Nothing could be further from the truth. Before you panic, allow us to explain. As long as you believed that help in coping with the existence of your personal fears was the best you could hope for, then that is indeed all that this beloved angel, this magnificent being of Light, could do for you. And this is what we mean by context. In a context of acceptance of the existence of fear overall, there are definite limits about what can be done, and the extent to which this planet can receive help.

In other words, if we, as a collective voice of humanity, are not asking for the complete elimination of fear, pain, death, and suffering, then those who would help us are limited by whatever we are willing to tolerate. Archangel Michael is here to eliminate the *source* of all fear. Period. Not to merely help us with it, not to justify it, and not to help us learn to accept and deal with it. All of those ideas presuppose that fear is supposed to be here, and that it is a legitimate part of our reality. It isn't. Fear exists as the experience of the absence of God. How in the world could there be anything legitimate or real about that?

In discussing this subject on a macro level of the existence of the finite Universe, rather than on the micro level of one individual's personal problems, there is another trick of the ego that you should be aware of. The ego is very fond of taking the fact that death, violence, pain, and suffering exist, and the ego blames it on the behavior of human beings. This is ridiculous because all of these things exist in the animal kingdom as well. The ego wants us to blame each other and make it a behavioral issue because that is a great way to start more wars and violence, and produce even more repression and control. This has the effect of producing even more death, more suffering, more pain, etc. Do you get the idea? The only thing that benefits is the ego, which has cleverly found a way to get humanity to energetically fund the environment of duality that it needs to survive, by continuing to battle each other.

Archangel Michael is 100 percent clear about what needs to happen here. There is no ambiguity in his mind whatsoever, but it takes a cocreative effort on the part of those human beings who are willing to live as active, cocreative participants. This is as simple as acknowledging the truth about what is in our hearts. We who live on this planet need to be equally as clear about what really matters to us so that we can ask for that and intend it. There is no power in the Universe that will interfere with our freedom to choose. If we want to continue to live in this finite Universe, then that manifestation can always go on. We can continue to make excuses for it, justify it, and tell ourselves that it is one great learning experience. Or we can stop lying to ourselves by saying that this is all okay with us when there is nothing in our heart of hearts that indicates that this is so.

This is our moment of truth. Our day of reckoning. As our planet continues to spiral out of control, when it comes to all of these things that we really don't want, we are faced with a choice of immense proportions. Are we going to be honest about what is in our hearts? Are we going to finally say enough is enough?

So let us now speak directly about heaven, and why it is such a universally understood idea. Heaven is not a place that exists up in the sky. Heaven is just another word for the Real World and the Real Universe. The experience of this is right behind our hearts. We already know this experience, as it is where we already live, as we pass our days in total slumber while we dream in this illusionary world. The dream includes living and dying as we explore the finite kingdom set in motion by the first, original lie. We are experiencing a waking dream, where we experience ourselves as wide-awake, yet we know in our bones that something is terribly, terribly wrong. Why don't we know who we are?

Why don't we know why we're here? Why are there so many questions, and where is God anyway? And what are these impossible things called violence and death, and why are they happening at all? So we answer our own questions, and then bury our heads in the sands of time, hoping that it will all be resolved by some unforeseen miracle.

The miracle is here, dearest friends. The miracle is evident in the fact that such words can now be written. The doors of our hearts are finally beginning to open, and we are collectively attuning to that which is the Light. Heaven is here, and it has always been so. Perhaps we have finally become ready to wake up to that fact.

CHAPTER 7

Prosperity

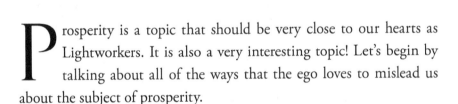

Prosperity is a topic that should be very close to our hearts as Lightworkers. It is also a very interesting topic! Let's begin by talking about all of the ways that the ego loves to mislead us about the subject of prosperity.

Like everything else in the domain of the ego, prosperity is erroneously defined. According to the ego, everything about prosperity is limited and finite. This is ironic when you consider the definition of the word. Prosperity denotes unlimited abundance. It has a connotation of expansion and ease. So why does the ego pretend that everything about it is so difficult and unattainable? Why does it get presented as something so scarce? In truth, prosperity is available as a worldwide phenomenon because it exists as a principle, not a thing. But the ego does not want you to know this. It would rather have you believe that it is like the pieces of a very limited pie, where there is only so much to go around.

In truth, prosperity is one of the many attributes of the Infinite. One of the most exciting things about the Real World is that there is no such thing as trying to "get" something against all odds. There simply are no odds against it! Infinite abundance, Infinite God, and Infinite Love are all one and the same. It makes absolutely no sense to think that there could ever be struggle. In order to have struggle, you have to have something always working against you, which is what we have here in the finite world. On Earth, we tend to believe that struggling against this "something," whatever it is, is the entire point of the matter. Can we overcome that "something" in our lives? Most of the time, the answer is no. So we learn to do the best we can with what we have.

Now the ego has taught us to make poverty a spiritual quest. The ego has told us that God *loves* lack and poverty. This is kind of funny because it is like saying that God does not want to expand, and instead prefers withdrawal. Can you imagine God behaving like some kind of a miser who hoards his beneficence and is reluctant to support anyone? Once again, the ego provides us with another cartoon-like explanation!

Let us ask ourselves why the ego would want so much for us to believe in poverty as a spiritual quest and as a way to please God. What do you think happens when the people of the world live in poverty, starvation, and lack? More pain and suffering, of course! Lots of despair, hopelessness, and desolation. And lots more death and violence, too. Do you remember why the ego likes and needs this desperate state of affairs? You guessed it. The ego needs this kind of environment in order to survive.

There is another benefit for the ego in an environment of poverty and lack. Such an environment contributes greatly to greater alienation from God. After all, how can you deeply trust something called God when that very same God is standing by and watching your children starve to death? The more alienated and distrustful human beings are of

God, the more likely they are to consider the ego's ramblings. Especially when the ego seems to be so ever-present, and God is nowhere to be found. Who do you think people are going to think their friend is? Why, the ever-present ego, of course.

But it's worse than just being a friend. The ego actually has you convinced that *you* are *it*. Think about this for a moment. In truth, it has been said many times that you and God are one and the same. How can it be otherwise if God is indeed infinite? It has been said that you are an expression of God in form.

But we don't really believe that here on Earth, do we? We might pay it lip service, but let's face it. Where's the evidence? The ego has eclipsed our real selves with an artificial version of our real personalities. This artificial version has all the hallmarks of the finite. It possesses every single manifestation of duality. Good/bad, happy/sad, rich/poor, healthy/sick, peaceful/angry, you name it. The list goes on and on. We are so entrenched in our artificial personalities created by the ego that we falsely believe that going against the ego is like going against ourselves.

Let us examine prosperity as a principle rather than something as silly as piles of money. The ego wants us to think of it as piles of money so we can fight about it amongst ourselves and struggle over who has more, and why they got it. More conflict, right?

God is infinite and exists as a manifestation of infinite abundance. They are one and the same. You can tell that this is true just by observing the unlimited nature of the known Universe. Can you imagine if the Universe had to be created by buying things with a limited amount of money? Wow! That would be something else, wouldn't it? First of all, where would the money come from? Who would organize it, and who would tell God that he/she couldn't have it? Unless God was willing to work for it, of course. And who would be in charge of that big bank in the sky? Do you see how preposterous this is?

Yet this is what we live here every single day. Now we are not going to get rid of money anytime soon; that's for sure. But it would behoove us to remember that it is just money. In reality, it has nothing to do with prosperity. Before you find yourself getting thoroughly confused, let us take a closer look at what money really is on this planet.

Money is merely a measurement of exchange. That's all! It's just a measurement. Kind of like a financial ruler. It can be measured with gold, it can be measured with pieces of paper, or it can even be measured with sticks, if everyone agreed to that. Currently, it is mostly measured with numbers. Just numbers. Like those things you learned about in school. 1, 2, 3, 4, 5, 6, 7, 8, 9, and 0. Those simple figures are all there is to the physical substance of money. What in the world do a bunch of numbers used to measure something have to do with prosperity and abundance? It is important that we take things literally in order to break the spell of intimidation about money, which only undermines our understanding of prosperity.

We tend to be intimidated about money because the use of those numbers is tightly controlled. But that fact should not influence our perspectives about prosperity. So here is where we can make a profound shift in consciousness. Prosperity is better understood as a verb than as a noun. It exists as the understanding of certain principles about how the Universe works. The dictionary would have you believe that prosperity is a noun, which defines a certain state of having already acquired enormous wealth. But prosperity is really about openness and trust. It is about understanding your interdependent role in the world and in the Universe.

This is a key understanding for any lightworker. Let us explain this more clearly by telling a story. Let's say there is a woman named Jan. Jan has a regular job, and goes to work five or six days a week. As a result of her work, Jan receives a paycheck, which helps her pay her bills and generally live her life. Her job represents an open door to a particular flow of money. This flow may be fixed, or it may have the ability to expand, depending on the job. The important thing is that Jan understands that her job represents a channel through which money can flow. If Jan wants more money, all she has to do is switch to a wider channel, or add another channel to her current one.

If Jan can see this as a channel rather than as a job, she can relax and surrender more easily to that flow. She will not need to expend unnecessary energy through tension and stress, and she will have a much more positive outlook. Her positive outlook will help her increase her flow of money since she is not fighting to get it anymore. The interdependent part is easy to see because wherever Jan is successful in her job, the success expands to benefit someone else.

That story represents the baseline in many people's lives. From here, you can expand further. Let's say that Jan has always had a feeling that she is here on Earth to do something very special, but she does not know what it is. Maybe she has been psychic all her life or perhaps extremely intuitive. Perhaps she is an artist or someone who is inspired to help children. Perhaps she just wants to help people in general, but she doesn't know how. If Jan tries to "think" of what to do, she will probably come up empty. That's because she would be relying on the ego to advise her, and we already know that the ego wants to keep everything intact in terms of her false identity. The ego, as you remember, is never a source of inspiration. It exists as more of a fixed program.

Jan could stop here and spend her life with this background nagging that there is something more for her to do, without ever being able to act on that feeling in a practical way. At that point of feeling stuck, Jan could potentially widen her experience of knowledge about the interrelationship between work and prosperity overall.

We as humans have an innate understanding about prosperity, as we are defining it. It is the paralyzed mindset of the ego that prevents us from recognizing that natural understanding and being able to act on it. So let us use this same story to elaborate on how that can change.

Prosperity always includes an element of interdependence in the world, and cocreatorship in the Universe. It exists as the natural synthesis of these elements in action. Going back to our story, let us remember that Jan, like everyone else, has guides and angels working in conjunction with her to aid and help further her evolution, whether she is conscious of that fact or not. This represents the first element of cocreatorship in the Universe. These guides and angels also operate in a much larger context that integrates with planetary evolution and evolution of the Universe. All parties work in conjunction with one another as cocreators while always preserving the mandate of free will. No one in this picture is ever telling anyone what to do or trying to control anyone. All exists in a state of benevolent love and harmonious integration.

This state of affairs is so natural that it may be one of the reasons that Jan doesn't even notice it in her everyday waking state. If this sounds strange to you, notice that everything in nature operates this way. All elements in nature complement and harmonize with one another so beautifully that you mostly notice the overall effect rather than the details of who is doing what.

Human beings are a part of nature, whether we choose to recognize it or not. Just as in the garden, where fairies, gnomes, and various nature spirits help with the flourishing of plants and animals, humans also have a tremendous amount of divine help in the form of angels and guides. There is a natural synergy in how our guides work together. Jan's guides may work in harmonious integration with the guides of someone else who is doing the sort of work designed to inspire and awaken others. Jan may hear about a seminar or a healer or find a certain book, seemingly by happenstance. Any of these avenues might serve the purpose of introducing new thought or inspiration into her consciousness. This entire unfolding exists as a manifestation of prosperity in the Universe, of which our planet is an integral part.

Jan did not necessarily seek out these avenues directly, but there existed in her consciousness an open avenue or channel through which these events and ideas could flow. Her sincere desire to know made it possible for the harmonious weaving together of certain events and their timing to yield something that she didn't have before. These events could then set up new tracks of consciousness that could likewise expand and unfold into even greater events in her life. It really depends on how open she is.

Now let us examine where the subject of money fits into prosperity as a component rather than as the main event. We'll go back to our story again to show how this can work. We shall put this in the context of experiences commonly had by lightworkers, as they find their paths of true purpose in the world.

Let's suppose that Jan finds herself awash in new information and new experiences of a higher, more expanded level of consciousness. In so doing, she begins to realize what her true calling may be. But she has never done anything about that calling before, and she has no idea how to integrate it into the life she has right now. The first item that will come into question is her job. That job may appear to have nothing whatsoever to do with her new sense of self and what she feels called to do.

What do you think the ego is going to do at this point? Create a perception of conflict, of course. It will likely go in one of two directions. The first thing that it will probably say is that the job is just too overwhelming and too time consuming to leave room or energy for anything else. Therefore, the best solution, according to the ego, is for Jan to procrastinate until the "magical unicorns in the sky" fix everything for her. In the meantime, the ego will tell Jan to just watch TV or some other form of electronic detachment because she is tired after work, and she really needs a break. *Blah, blah, blah.* The ego will drone on, absorbing all the beautiful oxygen in her consciousness. This is the ego's way of shutting down all the open avenues of consciousness that are emerging and ending this wonderful manifestation of Universal prosperity that is beginning to unfold.

Another favorite trick of the ego is to create withdrawal in Jan by introducing doubt and judgment into the picture. It will tell her that there are already so many more experienced people doing the kind of work that she is contemplating. It will tell her that she will just look stupid and amateurish compared to all of these experts. Besides, the ego will say, why would anyone want to come to her when there are so many other, better people around? In case Jan hesitates to buy into this line of reasoning, the ego has another trick up its sleeve. It will suggest that she needs to take a whole bunch of workshops, read a whole bunch of books, and explore as many different teachers as she can possibly find just to be really *sure* she is ready to do something of her own.

Naturally this is the carrot-on-the-stick routine that the ego is famous for. Needless to say, the ego plans to never, ever be satisfied that Jan has done enough. There will always be one more seminar, one more book to read, and one more teacher to investigate before the ego will say it's enough. The ego has subtly changed Jan's motivation to learn, from that of a sincere, heartfelt desire and openness to go forward, to one of fear, hesitation, and holding back. The ego is now using learning as a means to procrastinate.

And the final, most famous trick of the ego to sabotage Jan's natural movement into her purpose and higher consciousness consists of the following. This is generally the last trick that the ego pulls out of its hat, when all else has failed. It will say, "You know, Jan, you are going to be so good at this, and so amazing, that you should just quit your job. Cold turkey. Just do it, Jan. Remember those magical unicorns that I told you about? Well, they are all set to just whisk money into your bank account, no questions asked. After all, Jan, don't you think that the Universe is going to take care of you? You should have more faith! Go ahead, Jan. Quit your job! Just do it."

The ego knows that this is just a lot of baloney, but it is really feeling threatened because Jan is seeming just a little too serious about actually wanting to take on her true purpose. The ego's real plan here is to shut down all of Jan's possible avenues of income, thereby crippling her from being able to do anything at all. Because Jan has never physically done anything to enact her purpose as an actual line of work, the ego knows that she cannot realistically replace the income of her long-standing job overnight. It hopes to crash her entire journey by convincing her to remove that current channel of income, knowing that she will be in no position to build a new avenue of income when she is desperate for money just to survive, eat, and put a roof over her head. The ego hopes that after this terrible experience, she will lose all confidence, give up on this stupid idea, go get another job, and watch TV to escape all memory of her "mistake." The ego's real agenda here is to remove *all* channels of income, prosperity, and the like in order to teach Jan to stay in the box of her former personality.

Now that we have exposed the ego's main tricks of sabotaging Jan's opportunity for Universal prosperity, let us see what this story might look like if Jan doesn't fall for any of it. The first thing that will happen is that Jan's consciousness will remain open and therefore available for true guidance. Much of such guidance does not happen on a conscious level; it unfolds as synchronous opportunities, meetings, and intuitive ideas. This again represents a channel of prosperity in these particular forms. The way that Jan can stay attuned and open to these divine channels is to stay in touch with her heart and remain in a positive, loving, and sincere place.

Jan may recognize that she needs further education in the area of her purpose, but she will approach this constructively and know when to take the next step. Her education will not be used as a way to avoid something. This is where a clear understanding of the principles of Universal prosperity can help Jan flourish and succeed in her new endeavors. Because her consciousness is evolving in new directions, she is becoming more in sync with the forces of prosperity in the Universe. She is able to open more and more channels of understanding and intuition, all of which can easily bypass the meandering notes of the ego's sabotaging advice, as she gains greater inner strength.

At some point, Jan will feel ready to plan and launch her new endeavor. She does not have to view her current job as interference in that process. Instead, she can view it as a gift in her life that is there to support her needs while she plans and grows the adventure of her purpose.

It is interesting that the ego always wants to place the conflict squarely in the middle of something as essential as a person's well-established source of income, when they are in the process of making such a transition. Isn't it curious that the ego never frames this as a conflict with watching TV, surfing the Internet and social media, hanging out with friends, or engaging in any other easily dispensable habit? The ego will never challenge your need to do any of these recreational activities. No, the ego would rather challenge the job that provides you with the physical means by which to live. That is what the ego will say is dispensable, not the TV. According to the ego, you can live without your stable, financial income, but you could *never* live without YouTube and texting your friends. Amazing, isn't it?

In understanding the principles of prosperity, Jan can view her job as an already existent channel of income. She can then view the creation of her new endeavor as an additional channel of income. It is best if she views both of these channels as being about more than just money. Prosperity is much wider than that. It includes consciousness, love, opportunity, and service. It includes ever-expanding contribution. It includes creativity and knowledge. It even includes positive relationships. It widens to the loving guidance and support that one can receive from angels, guides, and other beautiful forces of evolution that exist in the Universe. In short, it includes anything and everything that contributes to your expansion and evolution, and to the expansion and evolution of our planet and the Universe.

It is a mistake to think of prosperity as having only to do with money. Why is this? Because money is only one small part of a much larger, integrated system of creative principles, as they exist on Earth in our finite Universe. It is much more important to integrate and align with those principles so that your life can begin to flow in synergy with those patterns of evolution. The way to do this is to remain humble, open, and sincerely receptive with love in your heart. It is also important to be discerning about what is indeed divine guidance and opportunity, and the bad advice usually given by the ego.

If Jan is successful at her new endeavor, and it becomes clear that the expansion of that endeavor is requiring more and more space and time in her life, there will be an obvious and graceful point of transition where her job will naturally begin to seem obsolete. At that point, she has the option to make decisions about what she wants to fill her space and time with.

Of course, there are always exceptions to this scenario. Sometimes the forces in the Universe acting on your higher behalf may intervene in your current status quo by turning all of your plans and habits upside-down and messing up your entire game board in order to get your attention. But don't think for a moment that your "higher self" or true self is not in on these plans and fully sanctioning them. Sometimes this is a better course of action overall, and it can actually speed up the entire process.

The main thing to understand about prosperity is that if you focus only on money, it will be like planting a seed on top of concrete. It simply will not grow. Although money by definition is merely a form of measurement, that which it purports to measure is entirely real and natural. Remember what is behind the money. Behind the money is energy and substance. Money is simply a way to control the movement of that energy and substance, or to identify where and what it is. That is why there truly is no shortage. Any perceived shortages are more about how we frame the movement of such energy. But what is behind the money is very difficult to control because without a fixation on currency as a method of measurement, it will just naturally expand.

And finally, remember to view money like a seed that requires fertile ground in which to grow. The fertility that gives rise to physical prosperity and abundance contains many, many components. It may require education on a purely intellectual level. It may require certain skills. It almost always requires constructive relationships and the ability to understand the healthy need for interdependency in those relationships. It requires integrity, honesty, and the ability to adhere to the basic principles of light, love, and sincerity in one's life.

A fertile ground for abundance also requires open-mindedness and a willingness to learn. It requires discernment and the ability to know truth from fiction. But most of all, it requires love—sincere love and caring for one's fellow human beings and the world around us. This includes a sincere desire to help in whatever way your inspiration may lead you.

The ultimate irony about money is that you have to take your focus off it in order to enter the Universe of prosperity. Remember that money is only there to measure something. It is not the thing itself.

CHAPTER 8

Who You Are in the Universe

Now we are ready to talk about your center in life, and offer you an opportunity to completely shift from where you have probably been living in terms of what you may have assumed was your only option. The first thing to shift in this regard is the context in which you have viewed your life.

On planet Earth, we are basically unaware of the Universe around us. We live as though our existence on this planet is all there is. This produces an immense distortion in our perspective, which we have no way of noticing because in this type of isolation, there is nothing else to see except our highly limited picture.

Your infinite self knows better than this, but unless that self becomes fully conscious on this planet, nothing will appreciably change. So let us start with a full acknowledgement that we do indeed reside in a vast, incomprehensibly large Universe. We do not have to physically know the entire map of the cosmos in order to be fully conscious of this fact. It is more about a sensation of where we are in time and space. The first thing to note is that we are definitely not limited to this tiny box called our finite perception of planet Earth.

Unfortunately, most human beings do not consider any of this an issue. They are content to believe that our universe of experience consists mainly of Earth. They might include the existence of the moon in this, but only as something that we observe from afar. As for the rest of it, they will generally not acknowledge the existence of much else, unless science points it out to them. And science does not have the capacity to point out very much at all. So if you plan to wait around for science to sanction the existence of everything out there, you could be waiting around for quite a few lifetimes.

Now it goes without saying that we can easily agree that the Universe is big, as an intellectual concept. But that is not what we are talking about. We are talking about the possibility of a visceral, real, physical, and energetic experience of this vast cosmos that we live in—without a spaceship. Don't you find it curious that we don't have that already? After all, we actually *do* live in space.

So many people inadvertently view space as something "out there." In fact, it is even called outer space. It is basically seen as something that has nothing whatsoever to do with our everyday lives. Yet it has everything to do with our everyday lives. How could it not? Do you actually believe that it simply doesn't exist just because we are physically blind and ignorant to how much this is all directly related to us personally?

That idea or false belief is once again directly related to the ego. To know why this is, it is important to understand the language of the ego. The ego can only speak in linear sentences, where words are strung together one at a time. Each word represents a thing, a concept, or an action that has already been known and experienced by people on this Earth, in its very tiny history of human existence. It basically takes the ego eons of time to learn anything new, and even longer to accept it. The ego simply will not acknowledge anything that has not first passed through its linear processing system, and then managed to fit in with its already tiny worldview.

This galaxy is far too big for the ego to absorb and comprehend, never mind the entire Universe. It still struggles with our solar system, for heaven's sake. To the ego, unless you are a planetary scientist or astrophysicist, any mention of our solar system probably brings to mind a cardboard mobile with circles dangling from it, the kind you saw in science class when you were forced to go to school.

The ego is all about control. It wants to control your entire perception of everything. If what you perceive and experience is outside of the ego's domain of existence, then it will cut off that perception and say that it doesn't exist. And let's not forget that the ego is a veritable fortress of excuses and reasons why. Justification is never a problem for the always-on-guard sentry of the ego.

We speak so much about the nature of the ego because unless you understand the difference between it and your real self, you will always be trapped inside of the dream world that it fully and completely protects. You will continue to think that the ego is you and then wonder why you feel so frustrated with no way out. Understanding the nature of the ego and its makeup is the only way to open your eyes and give you a chance to free yourself from the enormous limitations that it imposes upon you and your existence.

God did not create the ego. The ego is merely a byproduct of the first, original lie, which also exists as the original source of fear. If fear is an experience of the absence of God, then you should understand that this is a direct result of that first, original lie called "I am *not* God." The ego manifests as a default personality structure in an impossible world where there exists the illusionary experience of "God is *not* here." Thus such an experience can only be said to be the manifestation of a dream. The real you cannot operate in this dream world; therefore, an alternate you manifests in the form of the ego to effectively operate and mirror the basic duality that forms the foundation of this place. This is why you can feel so confused much of the time. This is why it sometimes feels like there are so many opposing viewpoints that live inside your consciousness.

Why do you suppose we would suggest that the real you cannot operate in the dream world of the ego? It is because there are far too many conditions and limitations that must be preserved in order for that world to continue to exist. The finite world is structured on a principle of duality where nothing is real and everything is an illusion. In truth, there is no such thing as good *and* evil where God is perceived as a finite thing, no matter how big that perception may be. As long as there is one tiny molecule that is perceived as a place where God is *not*, the entire Universe becomes a manifesting, finite illusion in your perception. The ego filters your natural perception of Oneness and splits it into two things to effectively mirror the foundational principle of this finite world.

So the real task at hand is to wake up to the presence of our true selves. To settle for this as a belief or conceptual knowing is utterly insufficient. In that case, it will merely sit at the back of our minds for some future date when we believe that it will be mysteriously activated, through no special act of our own. This is simply not the case. If it were, it would have happened long before now.

Let us begin this process of waking up by allowing ourselves to feel the physical existence of the Universe that lives all around us. There is an enormous energy of stars and stellar organizations of matter, all of which exude their own powerful auras. There are inter-dimensional phenomena that literally dwarf this tiny planet out of existence, in terms of sheer size.

Yet in spite of their presence of utterly massive proportions, these phenomena are also tiny when compared to something else. It is not at all important for our tiny physical brains to comprehend all of this. It is important to remember that our brains are really only designed for this world alone, and for the miniscule amount of matter in space that might be directly related to us. To try to use our earthly brains to comprehend the entire Universe would be futile and rather silly. So give your brain a rest, and allow your true Intelligence Factor to assist you here.

The Intelligence Factor also cannot be comprehended by the linear, Earth mind, and fortunately it doesn't have to be. The Intelligence Factor is perfectly capable of functioning on its own, without any need to be processed through a finite reality of experience.

The reason that we propose asking you to open up and feel the presence of our vast, interstellar Universe is to allow your physical body to attune to something much bigger than its everyday existence on Earth. It is vitally important to remember that our physical bodies indeed live in space. Just because we are on a planet that supports the unique makeup and structure of our physical selves, that in no way negates the fact that every moment that we are alive, we are indeed space dwellers in this enormous Universe.

One of the first things that you will have to be willing to do is to temporarily discard everything you have heard about the vast distances in space, along with the assumptions that because these distances are so vast, they couldn't possibly have anything to do with us. Especially throw away the idea of light years as a means of measuring such distances. This idea only reinforces the idea that everything revolves around our perception of Earth.

The matter that makes up your entire physical body is actually interstellar matter. This matter is activated by our sun, and it is also influenced by inter-universal, interstellar events that are unbeknownst to us on any conscious level. Many of these events could never be recognized or measured by any technology that we possess or by any that could be developed here in the future.

So, on a physical level, your body is extremely attuned to and is dependent upon these interstellar events. Imagine how tiny this Earth really is. It exists as barely a speck, in the shape of a microscopic sphere. How big do you think the energy field of Earth really is when compared to a phenomenon that is more than many trillions of times bigger than this tiny sphere? And that numerical example is still quite small. How big is one person's tiny energy field when compared to that of our whole planet? We are pointing this out to show you that the idea of physical distance is not really a factor. It is much more useful to consider the sheer size and magnitude of all of these interrelated energy fields combined, of which our own tiny planet is definitely a part.

Isn't it ironic, given these facts, that we here on Earth tend to view everything as a shortage of energy? What do you suppose might happen if you practice opening up to these vast fields of powerful, interstellar energies and their absolutely *huge* auras? Can you allow yourself to be consciously touched by that which already touches you? Remember, you do not have to be able to name and identify everything in the Universe in finite earthly terms in order to exist in relationship to those things. There are not enough words and concepts in all of the Earth languages combined, to even scratch the surface of such an idea. Just because you do not know the name and location of a particular star, does that mean that this star does not exist? The ego would like you to think so, and it will certainly have you behave accordingly.

If you believe that your identity lies inside of your teeny, tiny physical Earth embodiment, then all of these proposals will seem overwhelming, and to the ego, entirely unnecessary. The ego is incapable of fathoming anything outside of its tiny, tiny, little framework of existence. You should remember this the next time you are tempted to regard the ego as such a high authority in your life.

The idea of consciously connecting with the massive expanse of the entire physical Universe is important because it represents a first step of you beginning to take full command of your existence in this Universe. It represents you saying no to the ego. Believe it or not, you do have that right!

You do not need a spaceship to live in this Universe. You are already here. No matter where any physical spaceship may take you, you will still be no more *here* than you are right now. So what if you were to make it to Mars? Relatively speaking, that planet is closer to Earth than one skin cell on your hand is to the cell right next to it. It is closer to Earth than a single electron is to another in the very same atom on your skin. The entire galaxy is as close as your own backyard. And a neighboring galaxy is as close as a bird flying over a tree in that backyard.

So far, we have only spoken of the physical Universe that exists in the same dimension of time and space that we are familiar with. Think about the primitive way in which we measure time. Everything is measured based upon a single rotation of our planet. We have no idea whatsoever about galactic time, intergalactic time, and interstellar time. And even those ideas are incredibly elementary.

Now consider for a moment the fact that there are multiple dimensions of time and space, again on a physical level. There are hidden pathways to different realities all over the Universe. We really want you to understand the insanity of the bizarre and commonly held belief that Earth sets the standard for the existence of all else in the cosmos.

The fact is that if you are 100 percent identified with your tiny existence here on planet Earth, then there is no conceivable way for you to know who you are in the Universe. I hope we have succeeded in helping you begin to break up that conceptual straightjacket.

Now we would like to teach you an exercise to help you expand your consciousness in a way that promotes your freedom from this conceptual morass of highly limited perception.

You can begin by viewing this as a meditation of sorts, since that is what you are most familiar with. Sit in a quiet space and contemplate the fact that you are seated on a sphere that is suspended in unlimited space. There is no solid foundation of any kind underneath this sphere that is holding it up. In fact, you don't really know if your body is facing up, down, or sideways because the Universe has no boundaries of that nature. You could make the sun your point of reference, but where does that lead? Even if you could say that the sun has a reference point from inside the galaxy, you really have no idea about how this galaxy is situated overall. And what if the reference points don't even exist in this dimension? We feel such a need for all of these identifiable reference points because the ego needs that to feel secure.

But you, as an infinite being, need no such reference points. You are wholly aware of where every single thing lies in the entire Universe. You are already touching it.

Now allow yourself to open up. Open up and welcome in the consciousness and energy of the cosmos in which you live.

One other point should be stated here as an aside. We are embarking on a real experience of the Real Universe, which means that only Love exists here. We allow no room whatsoever for any illusions of duality, fear, and all of its accompanying illusions. And here we should also point out that there is indeed a Real Earth. This is the Earth that you have probably seen in what you thought was only your imagination. This Earth actually exists in the Real World. There is no violence here, and there is no hate. Living beings do not eat other living beings in order to survive. Death is not the food for living. In fact, there is no death here and no such thing as reproduction. It isn't necessary. There is only the profound beauty that you see here every day in nature, without the duality and without the fear. The Real Earth is indeed the paradise that you have always suspected this one should be. And that is only a tiny glimpse of the tremendous beauty and Love that exists throughout this entire Real Universe.

And lest you think that this Real Earth exists in some etheric realm of dreams, think again. We, on this false planetary experience, are the ones living in a dream. The Real Earth is more real than any of your physical senses could ever imagine. Its substance is so great, and its light so strong, that nothing could ever threaten its existence. There is no such thing as threat of any kind in the Real World of Omnipresent Love.

This Real Universe of which we speak does not exist in the familiar realm of "after-death" that you hear so much about. Please do not imagine that death is the road to that of which we speak. Nothing could be further from the truth. There is no death in the Real Universe, and likewise there is no place to go after it because it doesn't exist.

As you open up to the Real Universe, of which you are a part, remember that in truth, you are already here. You already exist as the unchanging infinite. This is very easy to see, if you take a moment to notice a few things. Look into your own eyes, without a mirror. Look at your experience from within. You will notice that although your physical face may change over the years, that you, yourself, never do. You do not need to look in a mirror to recognize yourself. You always know that you are *you*, no matter where you are or what you are doing. You do not need to keep checking in a mirror to make sure that you are seeing yourself.

If you really were your physical body, then why wouldn't you freak out anytime that body goes through changes? And it does go through many changes. How come you don't panic and go running around looking for yourself when your body looks different than before? It's because you are forever rooted inside your infinite self. And you know that. No one has to tell you this. Yet you will go around erroneously stating things like, "I am fat. I used to be thin" or "I am sick. I used to be healthy." The truth is that you are none of those things that are defined by this ever-present duality. You are experiencing a massive, collective dream where everything exists by way of its opposite.

So now we invite you to wake up and rejoin the Real Universe of Infinite Love. We invite you to remember who you are, the Real You that you live with every day, but wholly ignore in favor of the ego—your substitute self.

Who you are in this Universe is not something to be attained. It already is. All that is required is your own acknowledgement of such. Take command in the Truth of who you are. Take command of your life in this Universe once again. You are a loving being of Omnipresent Truth. You are a loving extension of the arms and heart of God itself. Embrace yourself. Embrace your life. Your life is not limited to this microscopic, planetary sphere. The entire Universe has been created just for you. Explore your true existence. Explore the Love. Remember who you are.

CHAPTER 9

Into the Light

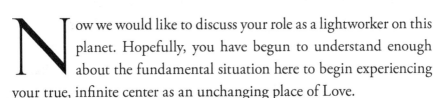

Now we would like to discuss your role as a lightworker on this planet. Hopefully, you have begun to understand enough about the fundamental situation here to begin experiencing your true, infinite center as an unchanging place of Love.

There are many physical roles that a lightworker can embark upon, but we shall not get into too many specifics about that since you probably already have some idea of what that means to you. If not, there are more than enough resources out there to learn more about whatever avenue you may feel attracted to.

Instead, we are more interested in offering you a greater context for your work and your physical presence on this Earth. The greatest challenge for any lightworker is to find some way to be conscious about his or her own presence from the other side of this duality that is manifesting on Earth and in the finite Universe. It is one thing to have a theory or belief about what this means, and it is quite another to experience it. Yet experiencing it is necessary if you are to achieve the power, clarity, and effectiveness that you may desire in all of your actions.

The first thing that we suggest is that you go to a place inside of yourself that is prior to whatever journeys you may have embarked upon in the realm of reincarnation and passing from one finite lifetime to another, to another, to another, etc. The second thing that we suggest is that you consider suspending all notions about old souls, advanced souls, evolved souls, and any other hierarchical ideas that you may have been exploring. All of these ideas exist in the finite, and they are a manifestation of many different paths in the exact same situation. We are interested in helping you out of this situation altogether.

The ego doesn't want you to know that there is something real beyond all of this because such a reality is transcendent of the ego's ability to manifest. So it will convince you that all of these seemingly endless outlets for experience in the finite Universe are the way to go. After all, what more could there be? The ego will suggest that God wants you to follow this inter-dimensional "yellow brick road" that endlessly winds throughout the finite Universe for untold eons of time.

It is understood that you have a particular interest in planet Earth, or you wouldn't be here. Maybe that interest is related to many prior lifetimes here, and this lifetime is one more leg on that entire journey. Maybe you have a deeper interest in helping to end the suffering here or in doing something to alleviate it in some way. Maybe you have a clear sense of mission and purpose here, and you wish to help others raise their level of consciousness overall. Some may be focused on the planet itself and its wealth of other life forms found in nature. Or perhaps you are just feeling frustrated or so despondent that you have no idea what the heck is going on here!

Whatever the case, everyone can benefit from reorienting his or her center of self to that which lies behind the veil. This is important because it will provide you with the necessary stability to navigate your consciousness through what is becoming an increasingly volatile situation on Earth. The place from which to begin this reorientation is to recognize consciously that you live with an ever-present experience that you exist, and that you are, indeed, alive. Remember that this experience is so familiar, so constant, that you may overlook it entirely. Your finite mind is generally looking to record duality, and it doesn't notice or record that which is constant. It will definitely take some effort at acknowledgement on your part. Remember to look to the heart for this experience instead of the mind.

Secondly, try to always remember your place in this Universe. Even though the entire world is preoccupied with Earth circumstances alone, always remember that you are part of a much wider cosmos. This is all about becoming re-situated in how you experience your life. In any duality, there exists an ongoing state of change, most of which will appear to be out of your control. To avoid losing your bearings, remind yourself that you are perpetually sourced in that which is constant.

These ideas will help you know where to start in your perspective. Always look for a real experience of yourself, no matter how small. It is definitely there, whether you are currently conscious of it or not. You do not have to create it. You simply have to acknowledge it consciously. The impediment that you may feel you are dealing with is mostly one of habit. Which habit? The one of relying on the mind and the ego for all of your perceptual information. Relying on the mind and the ego in order to experience your true self is like relying on a toaster to pick up an Internet signal for your computer. It's not going to happen.

Of course, when it doesn't happen, the ego will tell you that it proves that your "real self" doesn't exist. This will be followed by the ego letting you know that the only "self" you can experience is the one that the ego defines. You will know that this is happening when the ego proceeds to tell you how inadequate you are—and how all of this stuff is impossible for you anyway. Would you believe your toaster if it told you that there was no such thing as an Internet signal simply because the toaster could not pick it up? The next thing the toaster would say, if it were like the ego, is that your computer will never work and the fact that there is no such thing as a signal proves it. So always remember that the heart is where you will find yourself. Not the head. The head is the interpreter. The heart is the real thing.

It is very important in this world to learn how to use your innate faculties in a way that serves you as an infinite being. Mostly, you have been taught to use your faculties in a way that only serves the perpetuation of the finite. *You* are what animates the body. The body does not animate you. This is the first, most important thing to recognize. When you understand that, you will learn to see your body as an instrument rather than as the sole basis for your existence. This is the first step to being consciously in command. You can never be in command if you believe that the body is here to control you and define you. This is a dangerous thought anyway because if the body is sick, injured, or ultimately perishes, you will think that such things are really happening to you. In truth, such things are merely another common manifestation of what happens in the finite, where all things appear to have a beginning and an end.

You, yourself, can never be hurt, killed, or injured. Although you have probably experienced such things if you have traversed from lifetime to lifetime, what is actually happening is that you are experiencing your entire existence through the filter of a finite dream, in the form of a physical, finite embodiment. So the entire body acts as a filter to your experience of the Universe.

It is necessary to have a physical, finite body if you wish to be present on planet Earth and be physically functional here. If you have a positive purpose here, your body is really a gift because it allows you to enact that purpose in a way that makes a difference. This is why it is always a good idea to seek some form of mastery regarding that embodiment. Now mastery should not be confused with control.

Control is restrictive and based upon fear. Mastery is about finding harmony and a positive, loving relationship with the body. It has to do with understanding the body and learning to integrate with its systems in a way that supports the body and enlivens it with love. Then it is able to function as an extension of your true, infinite self rather than as a confused victim of the ego.

Now that we have discussed your infinite self, and your physical body as an instrument or an extension of that true self, let us discuss your physical place of residence, which is planet Earth. Earth exists as an extension of your physical Universe, which starts with your body. Your body and the planet exist as a unified field of energy. They are not really separate energetically. This is important to understand, especially if you are here to enact a purpose related to the transformation of this planetary sphere.

To what do we refer when we say the transformation of planet Earth? We refer to the transmutation of the dream. This is something that humanity as a whole has known about for eons. It has been written about, prophesied, and otherwise predicted. We know, as a species, that we are destined for the Garden of Eden. We know that there is definitely a place called home. We recognize that place in our thoughts, in our dreams, and in our divine imagination. We yearn for it in our prayers.

This place called home is where we will find ourselves when we awaken from this collective dream. We never left; we simply fell asleep. We remain unconscious as to who we really are and where we really live. This is a collective condition on a planet shared by all who reside here.

As was said before, there is the real Earth, which we are not awake to. Waking up refers to transmutation. Lightworkers are those who instinctively know that they are here to play a role in this awakening. It is not that our current planet will change into something else. It won't. In reality, it will cease to exist as we presently experience it. Why? Because this planet, as we currently know it in its false state of duality, is not real. There are principles present in our collective dream that simply cannot exist in truth.

For those who would question why God would create a world of pain and suffering, and the utterly needless experience of death, the answer is that God not only would not create such a thing, but cannot. It simply is not possible. For those who believe that there is something other than God, some evil force that would produce such things, you have fallen into the trap of believing in a dream that cannot exist. There is no *thing* other than God. And God is Infinite Love. Period.

It is time that we here on Earth experience all that exists in the Real World. It is not a boring world of Light with nothing whatsoever to do but float around. Floating around is for those who have crossed over after the experience of death, where they leave a part of themselves behind. This has nothing whatsoever to do with the Real World. The Real World is filled with Love. Filled with ineffable beauty. Filled with nature, places, and things you could never imagine. We refer to it as the Real World because it is so much more real than our currently manifesting dream. Our dream, the one that we wake up in every day, and the one that we imagine we die into as well, is etheric compared to reality.

There is not a single language on Earth, and not a single, physically spoken word that can refer to anything that exists in this Real World. Our languages are for the finite. Our languages describe what is, in reality, beside the point. The only real indicator that you have about the Real World is your beautiful, human heart.

Let us discuss what some of this awakening will include. No one knows what this looks like in time and space, by the way. You will not be able to place such a thing inside of our familiar space-time continuum. It will be necessary to accept that the ego knows nothing about any of this, and it has no capacity whatsoever to know. Since we are bringing up the subject of time, let us put that in perspective. Time, as we know it, refers to our planet's rotations and revolutions around the sun. Human beings will come and go, through life and death, in the context of those rotations and revolutions. Whether you are incarnate in a physical body, or off the planet in between lives here, the timing is still the Earth's. It should also be known that Earth's timing is directly tied into galactic timing, inter-dimensional timings that we cannot measure, and other factors that we have no conceptual knowledge of here.

Now it is time to discuss a few of the elements innate to the finite, and how those elements will, and are, reacting. You should know that in a world of duality, there will always be a powerful resistance to Oneness and to the Infinite. This is not about "evil," and it is not about something bad. In fact, the irony of this entire situation is that the so-called good *and* the bad will both react equally as negatively to Oneness. Why is that? It is because they both rely upon each other in order to exist. In a dualistic world, you only know that you are good by way of contrasting yourself with what you perceive as bad. This, of course, is always entirely relative. Everyone on Earth who is doing what many would refer to as bad actually believe that what they are doing is good. If you have one tribe that wants to slaughter another tribe, it is only because they believe that the other tribe is bad; therefore, removing them is a good thing. The tribe being slaughtered thinks the opposite, of course.

Be careful not to fall into the trap of good and bad. There is no such thing as either one. It is far too changeable. Love, on the other hand, is not related to good or bad. Love requires no judgment. It simply is. Conditional love, born of judgment, resides in the realm of good and bad. It is in no way related to Infinite Love.

As Infinite Love moves ever closer to our collective dream, the good and the bad will become highly polarized. You will begin to see, more and more, that it is possible to stand on the side of either one, and understand the rationale for each. Each side is likely to want full destruction of the other, and with very good reasons to back them up. This is what has been referred to as the battle of Armageddon.

Earth will go through many things during this time of polarization. There are all sorts of possible outcomes, but you would be wise not to fixate on any particular one. What happens here affects you whether you are living or not living. Therefore, it is wise to know where you stand overall, regardless of your current position in the Universe. That way, it won't matter where you are. This realization is actually part of your necessary awakening. It represents your ever-increasing ability to view yourself as immortally alive, whether in a body here or not.

Let us discuss what you might do to help facilitate this process. It is commonly known by those who are already engaged in a lightworker's kind of work, in whatever form, that a main objective is to bring more love and light into this planet and its energy fields. This is absolutely true, but let us suggest a slight shift in terms of how you perceive that idea. The only problem with this perspective is that it subtly implies that the light always comes from above or from the outside. This is akin to the ancient belief that heaven is in the sky.

Light emerges from within the heart—and from within each and every cell, molecule, and atom of your being. It radiates outward from within you. This exists as the natural order of things. Because you are a creator, you have the capacity to project Love from within you outward, in all directions. This takes absolutely no physical or energetic effort whatsoever. What it takes is a sincere effort to know who you are, and to be that Love. The ego will do everything in its power to eclipse that Love by distracting you with all of its survival agendas and trying to rope you into being afraid. But when you are in that Love, the ego has no power to reach you.

In being Love, all of your actions are imbued with Love. You effectively become a manifestation of Love, entering the planet and transmuting the dream. Light does not dispel the darkness. In truth, there is no darkness.

Remember, too, that you are not alone. The entire Universe is behind you and backs you up 100 percent. The dream is challenging, to be sure, but that is only because you perceive yourself to be a part of it. We are here to encourage you to be a part of the Real Universe rather than of the dream of Earth. It is true, of course, that you will need to function within the dream in order to effectively play your part in Earth's transformation. Can you function inside the dream without believing in it? In order to do so, you must remember who you are.

Earth's transformation is included in a much wider transformation of the entire Universe. There is a great deal of life involved. You have many, many friends in high places, as the saying goes. You probably already know some of them. This transition from dream to Reality was inevitable. There is simply no way that a finite version of reality can sustain itself indefinitely. The pressure of the Real World impinging on the illusionary world of death and destruction is simply too great to resist for any extended period. One can only place a hand over his or her eyes for so long; eventually the sun will sufficiently radiate its warmth and light, to the point where that hand will naturally give way to the sun's irresistible beauty and illumination.

PART 2
(Archangel Michael)

CHAPTER 10

The Nature of the Universe

Greetings! I am that which is known as Michael, and to many as Archangel Michael. To some, I am known simply as Mikhail. Let us begin at the very beginning, which ironically has nothing whatsoever to do with time.

"So what is the beginning?" you might ask. The beginning, in reality, exists as the ever-present and illustrious moment called Now. It is interesting, is it not, that you reside permanently in this moment, yet it appears to be that which is most unfamiliar to you, and most elusive. And it is primarily because of this mystery that you do not fully understand the Universe in which you live. All of your sciences begin in the so-called arena of time and space, and it is from there that your human species attempts to understand all that is. The problem with this approach is that it includes many, many false assumptions. For example, it presumes that God creates within the space-time spectrum. It doesn't.

"But, wait!" you might say. "How does that explain the very existence of life as we know it?"

Take note, dearest friends, of the fact that nearly all of your scriptures, in ancient as well as current writings, are fully aware that something exists here in a way that God did not intend. Now why is that important? It is important because how you hold that fact in your consciousness and the way in which it influences your perspective completely determine the outcome of your existence in Universal life. Notice that I did not say planetary life. Planetary life is all too short in its current form to accommodate the width and breadth of all that you must consider.

There is much debate, for example, about what must happen after one "dies." This perspective alone is erroneous, and can easily be proven to be so. "What will happen to me after I die?" If you can even contemplate that question, it is clear that you are aware of the fact that you don't. Otherwise, how do you explain the "you" in that sentence? Now this can be intimidating to some, due to the fact that they are completely unaware of who that "you" will be after this thing called death occurs. And if such a profound lack of awareness exists, then does that not call into question the "you" that you think you are right now? Does it not seem natural that your sense of who you are should expand throughout the Universe at a conscious level right now? And if it doesn't, then why not?

So this, dearest friends, is where we must begin if we are to embark upon any understanding whatsoever about the nature of the Universe in which you live. It begins, first and foremost, with waking up into an acknowledgement that you, yourself, must certainly be larger than the Earth-based circumstances in which you live. This understanding is vital because it is the only way that you can find any power in dealing with those Earth-based circumstances as they exist right now. And you are soon to find out, due to your rapidly advancing technology, that these Earth-based circumstances will not remain merely Earth-based a whole lot longer.

Let us take a moment to examine the current, most popular perspective of life on planet Earth. Mostly, it is a mystery that is fraught with many questions. *Why am I here? Where did I come from?* and *What am I supposed to be doing?*. And in relation to the surrounding physical space of the Universe, the larger questions persist. *Is there life out there?* and *Who made all this stuff, anyway?* Do you not find it strange that so many questions exist about things that should be so obvious? People are literally tormented by these questions for their entire lives. It is very unsettling to know so little about such utterly fundamental issues, such as who you are, where you are, and why. It is rather like being completely blind.

This lack of knowing produces fear. The fear then gives rise to any and all manner of answers. This is how the word "God" was created. The literal definition of the word *God* is the One who created all that is. This sounds wonderful, except for one thing. You don't experience it. And that is indeed the problem, is it not? It is a conceptual knowing, and therefore you tend to pray in the dark. It often feels like that, doesn't it? It can feel as though you doubt whether or not anyone hears you. What is the primary thing that produces this doubt? Lack of results, of course!

So in this tremendous void of experience, many temporary answers are generated. Why do I say temporary? Because they are not working, that's why. Rather than take that statement at face value, let us take a moment to examine that fact in the proverbial light of day.

Planet Earth is a violent planet. That is an indisputable fact. There is violence everywhere, and not just in the human realm of existence. There is a great deal of violence in what you refer to as the natural world. Did you not notice that in order for anything here to live, something else must die? It's called the food chain. How peculiar that the death of one thing actually contributes to the so-called life of another. That is, of course, until that thing must eventually die as well. So in this peculiar chain of events, it is ultimately death that makes life possible. And herein lies your first clue! "A clue to what?," you might ask. A clue to the fact that something could be very, very wrong with this picture. Yet there are those who already know this, aren't there? They are called radical vegetarians. "Don't eat anything with eyes!" they will tell you. "It's better to eat only plants. At least they can't see what you're doing." Now that is a noble gesture, indeed, and it is certainly born of a sincere desire to rectify the situation. But those who feel this way certainly know that it is not enough in terms of correcting the larger violence all around you. How many animals in the wild are not able to become vegetarians? But then this gets rationalized as "natural," and thus the confusion begins.

And what about all of the spiritual violence? Let us examine that for a moment, shall we? Religions are famous for their very creative solutions of slaughtering everyone who does not believe as they do. Naturally, this seems appropriate since Earth is clearly a violent place already. So why wouldn't this solution fit right in with God's plan? After all, according to many religions, God is very happy to punish you after death anyway, so why not speed up the process and do away with all those unbelievers? We're just helping God out, aren't we?

And this, of course, leads to the ancient subject of man's injustice to man. Why are human beings so cruel to one another? Philosophers have pondered this question for eons, and have basically come up with only one answer. Because people *feel* like it, that's why! Naturally the philosophers don't put it in such simple terms. They would be out of a job if they did. Instead, they ponder all the reasons *why* people may feel this way. In other words, they attempt to justify it. They do so by examining the circumstances in which these feelings to do harm to another may arise, and they attempt to explain how human beings react to those circumstances accordingly. This is all well and good, but it does nothing to solve the problem. And herein lies yet another clue. The fact that all of this violence is clearly perceived as a problem indicates that human beings are fully aware of the fact that something is indeed wrong with this picture!

Now we must examine what human beings have tried to do to correct this violent state of affairs. It starts with perspective. In order to act upon any set of circumstances, the mind will always produce a perspective or mental guideline about what is going on. From there, it will attempt to take action according to those guidelines. For the purpose of this dialogue, we will examine the spiritual perspective that is most common to humankind on this planetary Earth.

It starts with a belief that all of this violence is somehow God's will. And for those who no longer subscribe to the belief in God as a separate entity, this belief takes on a new form. *I, as a soul, wanted to have this experience for myself.* Now that belief works out really well, until such people find themselves in the throes of some horrific type of pain and suffering, in which case they will likely find themselves changing their minds rather quickly!

Sit back for a moment if you will, and try to picture this situation in an entirely neutral way. Imagine yourself standing back, away from the planet (much like an extraterrestrial might do), and allow yourself to get a real sense of the profound amount of violence, pain, and suffering going on. (For all of you positive thinkers, don't worry; this viewpoint is only temporary.) Now switch for a moment to what you know to be true in your heart. That God is Love. Pure and simple, isn't it? Except for one thing—it doesn't explain all the suffering. You see, you can't have it both ways. Either God is pure love, or it's not. If God has the capacity to sanction and create violence, pain, and suffering, then how do you explain your clear, unadulterated knowingness that God is love? And here is where the problem arises. The fear of not knowing the truth about God, not knowing the truth about oneself, and not knowing the truth about the Universe at large, produces a desperation to produce an answer—regardless of whether or not that answer makes any sense.

The mind says, "All of this must be God's will since we know, of course, that God is Omnipresent." This answer should immediately be recognized as flawed simply because it goes without saying that God/Love cannot beget pain and suffering. But because the mind is desperate for an answer—any answer—it simply chooses to overlook this glaringly obvious fact. Instead, it looks for new and better ways to justify this answer. "Well, since God can't be bad, it must be humans that are bad." The only problem with this line of reasoning is that God is Omnipresent, remember? That means 100 percent present in humans, too. So you are back to the same dilemma again.

A simpler way to look at this is as follows. God is Infinite Love. The key word here is *infinite*. In which case there can be no such thing as finite, correct? That is, if infinite really means infinite, which of course, it does! So how then do you explain the existence of this experience called finite?

Have you ever contemplated something known as the first original lie? And what is the nature of a lie after all? It is that which attempts to eclipse or to go against the truth. So the only possible lie that could be told about the infinite is to declare oneself *not* infinite! And thus is produced the illusion of the finite. For all lies are illusions, are they not? Now, I am fully aware of the difficulty that most finite beings have in declaring their very existence to be an illusion. So let us examine for a moment why that is. It is because you deem violence to be real. By what means do you do this? By declaring that that which can destroy something else bears the most evidence of its reality. By declaring that that which can destroy presents the greatest, most concrete evidence of its existence in your world.

The nature of the finite is to clash with itself. It is based solely on division. Ultimately, it is based on its original lie. "I am *not* infinite." This translates into, "I am *not* Love." This ultimately translates into another statement. "I am *not* God." And thus is born the illusion of the Antichrist, meaning that which goes against God. Some refer to it as the fallen angel. But I must inform you that there is no such thing as a so-called fallen angel, simply because there is no such thing as something that can exist by virtue of what it is *not*. Make sense?

Surely by now, someone is saying, "But Archangel Michael, we *do* exist in a finite dimension, don't we?" Well, in truth, you actually *don't* exist there. That is why you have so many questions. It is why you can't actually *see* anything and why you make up answers that don't make any sense. It is why you don't experience God and feel forced to settle for religion and philosophy instead. It is why you refer to your "higher self" and desperately try to bring it here, so that it will have some influence over your life. It is why you have compartmentalized the entire Universe in your mind's eye, in such a way as to explain your plight.

Let us talk for a moment about this notion of a higher self. In truth, there is no such thing as a higher self, or a self from which you are wholly displaced. This is merely another illusion of division as produced by the finite and the first, original lie of "I am *not*." But you cannot experience that higher self as *your* self in a land that is not infinite. Why? Because the higher self is *you* in infinite form! In that reality, there is no such thing as *not* infinite. Remember? Thus, you experience a profound separation.

There are also those who will argue, "But Archangel Michael, the finite Universe is huge! Therefore it must be valid, right?" Not necessarily. How big is your imagination, after all? Is it really that difficult to mathematically produce unlimited fractals of creation? It is still math, after all, and therefore it is clearly finite. It should be understood that the finite can easily surpass your mental capability to imagine it.

Why is all of this important? In the next chapter, we will examine exactly why this is so.

CHAPTER 11

Prayer

Let us now discuss why your explanation of what is going on in your world is so important. It is because your explanation produces a mental paradigm from which you will pray for help.

The fact that you are asking for help at all is, in and of itself, an indication that something is amiss here, wouldn't you agree? Mostly when people pray, they are asking for help and relief from something negative. That something negative can take the form of pain, suffering, grief, and an overall sense of difficulty with life itself. Sometimes the prayer exists as a request for more love in the world. But how can it be that more love is required when divine love is already infinite? And here again is where the explanations tend to go off the rails.

"Well," people say, "God is putting us through this because he/she/it loves us and wants us to learn." (Note that there is even indecision about what gender this God really is!) Some will say that God provided people with these bad experiences so that they would learn to better appreciate the good and not take it so for granted. Do you really need to lose your legs in order to appreciate them? Or how about losing a beloved family member? Is this really necessary in order to have the chance to eulogize them and *finally* let the world know how much you truly appreciated their presence? Is the nature of God such as to say, "Hmm ... I know how to help these people have a better experience. I'll take away that which they really love and need in order for them to *really* appreciate it!"? Really? So the *absence* of that which you love will actually breed more love for that thing or that person?

Now some people will say that there is value in the earthly struggles of humanity. They tell you that it will build strength and character. But shouldn't you already have that if you truly are created in the image and likeness of God? The bottom line is that all these explanations are totally fraught with confusion and discrepancies.

If we were to put all of these explanations in a giant basket, they would have one thing in common. They are all premised upon a belief that God/Infinite Love is somehow responsible for creating a violent world such as Earth, along with an equally violent universe. They all presuppose that the infinite and the finite can coexist.

What sort of prayers does a human being pray when that human being believes that God itself has ordained such a violent world—for what that person believes is a very good reason? This, my dearest friends, is a truly dangerous paradigm if you ever hope to restore that which is Infinite goodness and Love in this world of yours, and in your Universe.

Do not underestimate the absolute power of prayer to produce a result. All of the Infinite hears a prayer that emerges from a sincere heart. The problem in adequately responding to that prayer arises from the erroneous assumptions from which that prayer might emerge. Currently, the most prevalent of these assumptions is founded in the false belief that God/Love begets pain and suffering, and for a presupposed good reason. When this is the unconscious premise of your prayer, you will find yourself wholly limited in what it is that you can actually pray for. You will find yourself praying for relief from one specific circumstance, that may be yours alone. Or you might even enlarge the scale of your request to include help for a certain group of people who are suffering from a natural disaster.

These are noble prayers, to be sure, and I certainly do not advocate stopping such beautiful inquiries of love. But your world and your situation here require something much, much larger in terms of a response. Yet the response can only equal the magnitude of the prayer. And if the prayer is limited by a belief that God wants all of this suffering, then you find yourself in the role of a beggar rather than one who indeed sits on the right hand of God, because in truth, you are a manifestation of the Infinite yourself.

The purpose of this discourse is to provide you with a choice. And the choice may not be an easy one, although it is indeed the most desirable. One choice that you have is the one that you have already made. And that is the choice to believe that somehow all of this pain can be justified and explained away; therefore, your task is to either learn to live with it or to somehow better yourself because of it. The problem with this choice is that the events in your world are in the process of overtaking this form of rationale in such a way as to eclipse your ability to believe in this for very much longer. And thus I, Archangel Michael, have come to offer you another option. Whether or not you choose this option is entirely your prerogative. You will be equally loved by that which is divine, no matter what you choose to do.

"So what is this choice?" you might ask. The choice is simple. It starts with acknowledging what you know to be true in your heart. What your heart tells you, unequivocally so, about the truth about life in this Universe. That there should be no such thing as pain. That there should be no such thing as death. That there should exist only joy, creativity, love, and happiness. That there should be no such concept as health, because all exists in a state of wholly immortal enlightenment. And on and on it goes.

Ask your heart sometime what it really wants to tell you. Remove the censoring device that is only there to protect a false and erroneous belief. The belief that says that you, or God, or some sort of karmic regulation says that this pain and suffering is really necessary on some kind of "spiritual" level. The utterly false belief that true life can only be experienced in the finite, and that your immortal self sees this as highly advantageous. Do you know what the meaning of the word "finite" really is? That which has a beginning shall also have an end. Is this what your heart really wants when it comes to love?

Allow me to suggest to you an alternate form of prayer. For prayer is your greatest power. If you are willing to pray in true alignment with what your heart knows to be true, you will find yourself praying an altogether different set of prayers. Because your heart exists in a state of Oneness with Love and the Infinite, you will immediately see that your own personal plight cannot be adequately addressed in a void. You will understand that, first and foremost, your prayer must address the world. You will realize that your private form of pain exists in a larger context where pain is possible. Think for a moment of how powerful a prayer would be if it addressed the issue from the pure state of the heart with no compromise and no excuses for why the pain exists. Imagine what it would be like to give yourself permission to pray for the elimination of that which causes the possibility of pain in the first place. Can you allow yourself to experience that level of truth?

Some might see this as a matter of good behavior. *Can we please have everyone on Earth simply behave themselves and not cause any more trouble?* How about the notion of world peace? *Can we please get rid of all the weapons and stop all the wars?* Interesting how that prayer has never really worked out, has it? There may have been a temporary reprieve here and there, but overall war and the development of weapons is more active today than ever before. So when these prayers never really work out after thousands and thousands of years of trying, then the assumption that generally follows is that it is either the fault of the humans—or God simply believes that you deserve all of this suffering.

And next comes the guilt. "Well," people say, "we are clearly miserable failures as a species. Otherwise all of this praying would have yielded some result." Actually, your prayers have yielded *many* results, as those who have had them answered can readily attest. It is just that in terms of your main plight as a collective species, those results are far too small. So let us clarify one thing. Nothing in this Universe can change your plight unless you specifically ask for it and want it. You must want it with all your heart and soul. But if it does not occur to you to ask for it, there is little or nothing that can be done. As long as you continue to rationalize, excuse, and convince yourself that all of this suffering is God's will, then the best prayer that you can offer will be along the very limited lines of asking for help in coping with the situation.

Now let us talk about death. Definitely a taboo subject, right? And why is that? Death, you see, is ultimately a matter of physics. Unfortunately, those particular physics are produced by the existence of the first, original lie. The one that says, "I am *not* Infinite." Well, in that case, you are finite, and therefore something that can't really exist except as a manifestation of that lie.

All lies must have a beginning. Their beginning occurs the moment that one decides to eclipse the truth. All truth is infinite. To proclaim that one is not infinite is to generate an entire universe of finite matter, all of which is ultimately an illusion. And what do you think happens in this universe of finite matter? Lots of violence and lots of collision; everything in that finite world attempts to secure its own survival in a universe where death is always imminent. This happens at a microcosmic level of human existence, as well as at a macrocosmic level of solar systems and galaxies. We will not discuss the subject of extraterrestrials since you clearly have your hands full with your own planet.

Yet you need not worry about praying for your entire Universe. That subject is currently well outside of your range of perception. But why not begin by considering your own planetary plight? That is what your heart knows and what you will clearly see if you allow yourself to do so.

Let us now discuss the subject of prayer itself. What is prayer? Prayer is mostly known as an appeal to the Infinite by those who find themselves in finite situations. The core motivator for nearly all prayer is a recognized need for assistance in getting out of any particular situation. In this case, it would exist as a recognition that all is not as it should be in the realm of Love. Later in this discourse, we will discuss the ways in which the ego can erroneously influence one's desire to pray. But for now, let us concern ourselves only with the matters of the heart. The heart has a simple, one-pointed, and irrevocable direction in terms of its prayer. And that prayer exists as a perpetual desire to return to a state of Truth or Oneness. It wants only to know its true state of infinite love and to manifest the creation of that love throughout all of reality.

Did you know that you are a creator? On Earth, it may seem that you are primarily a survivor. How do you know? Because every day you wake up to the recognition that you are still alive. That is until you don't. Which makes life very precious, doesn't it? But isn't there something wrong with a situation that requires death in order to fully appreciate life?

I propose this simple truth to you. Why not allow your heart to speak its truth to you in a way that is unadulterated by any acquired beliefs? That truth may seem outlandish to you. Maybe even radical, as the heart informs you that all there is is Love, and that that is all you should experience. The heart has a great deal more to say, all of which is positive, loving, and beautiful. There is no suffering in the abode of the heart. The heart will never tell you that life is about overcoming pain and suffering. It will tell you that pain and suffering should not exist.

CHAPTER 12

Adam and Eve

Let us acknowledge up front that many people do not believe in the Garden of Eden and the story of Adam and Eve. That is not the point. The point is that the story of Adam and Eve is the perfect metaphor for humankind's plunge into a finite experience of reality.

The Garden of Eden clearly represents what I shall refer to as the Real World. What indeed is the Real World? It is that world that exists in an infinite state of being. In truth, the Real World is not a world of planets and stars, but it is indeed a world of Universes. A multidimensional Omniverse of purely infinite capacity to manifest and create. And it should be stated here that there exists no spoken language on Earth, conceptual or otherwise, that could ever touch a description of such a profound reality. It should likewise be understood that the authors of the story of Adam and Eve were speaking in a conceptual language reflective only of what was known on Earth at that time. Thus, it can only be construed as a vague metaphor.

It should also be known that the Real World is one of Infinite Love. There is no pain and suffering there. There is no such thing as death. Now some might erroneously construe this to mean that this is what is known as the famous etheric world of the so-called afterlife. Wrong! The afterlife is as much a part of the finite universe as physical life is. They are inextricably woven together, as those who have regular contact with this afterlife can readily attest. Notice the peculiar name that has been assigned to this realm. *Afterlife?* Hmmm ... very strange indeed! Hardly what one would refer to as a real world of any kind. For those that have loved ones currently residing in that realm, please do not take offense. Since your physical world is no more real than theirs is, it is all pretty much equal.

Why is there an "afterlife" anyway? Because wherever the illusion of death occurs, there must also be a place for such unfortunate souls to go. Why do I say unfortunate? Because there is simply no point to death, that's why. Have you ever wondered why death is often so violent? Have you ever wondered why it involves so much pain and suffering in order to get there? After all, couldn't you just decide to lie down one day and merely go into a permanently peaceful sleep? Why the violent end? Interesting question, isn't it? Later in this discourse, I will let you know why this subject will be important to contemplate.

But for now, let's get back to Adam and Eve. In the story, Adam represents that which is termed the male principle in human form. Eve represents the female principle. Male and female are always required for creation in the Universe as you know it. You can also refer to it as yin and yang or as the negative and positive charges found in the magnetic construct of atoms and molecules. Adam and Eve exist as the pure creative principles of yin and yang in that which is termed the infinite Universe in which human beings were meant to reside. This principle is so powerful that it is even found in every particle of finite matter as well. It simply cannot be erased.

For those who are wondering, this is not an issue of heterosexual versus homosexual. It has nothing to do with it. All people possess what is termed the yin and the yang. It is what holds your very molecules together. The magnetic force of creation. This force exists as the great equalizer in the Universe. It is beautiful, powerful, and filled with the very spark of life. So everyone can rejoice equally in its splendor!

So here we have Adam and Eve (the spark of creation) existing in the Garden of Eden (the Infinite Universe). They are surrounded by the infinite beauty of creation itself. According to the story, they are given "dominion" over this planetary creation. Technically speaking, this simply means that they have dominion over it because these principles are necessary to the manifestation and ongoing existence of this creation. If we are to examine these principles in human form as it states in the story, then we can also note that humanity is a creation with capabilities that far exceed the kingdoms of animals, plants, and the other elements of planetary development.

Now if there are any Bible scholars reading this (which is doubtful), understand that I am taking great liberties with this story, which, believe it or not, is not a sin! My only aim is to make a simple point.

In this garden, there is love, peace, and harmony. No one is killing each other because there is no death! All is infinite. Animals do not attack and eat one another. There is no food chain here. There is only love. And true beauty, which is the manifestation of Love itself. So overall, we could say that this garden represents the true nature of the Infinite Universe.

So here is where the story gets interesting. In this Universe, or garden of beauty, there exists something called *the tree of the knowledge of good and evil*. Pay close attention to that phrase! Adam and Eve are specifically told not to eat of the fruit of that tree. Let us be clear right off the bat. The fruit of that tree is *the first, original lie*. The first lie that begat all other lies and illusions. The lie called, "I am *not* infinite." Which, as we stated before, is not possible, which is what makes it a lie! Now what do you think happens if the yin and the yang, the first magnetic principles of all creation, eat the so-called fruit of that lie? "Eating the fruit" is a metaphor for taking that lie in and then producing creation from within that lie. You see, these principles cannot help but create. When absorbed into a lie, they will continue to create, although now the only thing they will create is illusion. After all, what else do you think is possible under such conditions? And, by the way, do you really think it is a big deal to create an entire finite Universe as a result of this? Of course not! Size is not an obstacle.

Now enter the serpent, which is the voice of that lie. Notice that the first thing the serpent does is to *justify* why Adam and Eve should partake of that fruit. Have you ever noticed that all lies have to be justified? They simply cannot stand on their own. Try to tell a lie without having a darn good reason to do so. Have you noticed that there is always a reason? So the serpent informs Eve that she should eat of this fruit because if she does, think of how *smart* she will become! (Enter the notion of time and space.) The serpent tells her how pleased she will be with the so-called positive results of that act. (Does this remind you of all the so-called good advice that the ego gives you? *Do this and great things will happen for you!* So you do it, only to find that the results are devastating. Sound familiar?) Basically the serpent is letting her know, erroneously of course, that the knowledge of evil will be a great idea! And if there is therefore such a thing as evil, then what does that make good? It makes it something that will forever vie against evil for power, of course! Thus is born the proverbial battle of good versus evil. Now doesn't this sound silly when you step back and look at it? What is the point, after all? It sounds more like a bad experiment that went awry.

The serpent also encourages Eve to eat of this fruit because of the "power" she will have. The creature tells her that her power will therefore be equal to God's. Now there is a very specific reason that the serpent says this. It is not just rhetoric! There are actually certain laws of physics that will be immediately created, which will provide the *illusion* of a power equal to God's. But it is all illusionary, you see. The lie called "I am *not* infinite" represents *resistance* to the Truth of that which is termed Infinite. The serpent's illusion is that its feigned ability to resist the Infinite by lying represents a power that is equal to the infinite. The only problem is, of course, that this entire charade doesn't exist at all!

So Eve believes the serpent's nonsense, and she gladly eats the fruit of the lie. Because she and Adam are one in their creative principle of who they are, naturally Adam is eating the fruit, as well. (For those of you who may think that this story is sexist by blaming Eve for the first mistake, that is also not true. Remember that the female principle is the receptive principle. Thus it is obvious that this lie would automatically seek out its ability to embed itself in this creative principle by entering at the female opening. It's not about choice; it's about physics.)

Once Adam and Eve have partaken of the fruit of the serpent's lie, everything changes immediately! Let the illusion begin. The first thing that happens is that they observe that they are "naked." Now what does this mean? Metaphorically speaking, it means that they are vulnerable. Vulnerable to what? Well, the Infinite, of course! Remember that they have eaten the fruit of the fundamental lie called "I am *not* Infinite."

Because they are still a creative force, they must manifest this lie. The only way to do so is to *resist* the truth that they are indeed infinite and that they are indeed a manifestation of God. In this resistance, "God" and the "Infinite" become their enemy. In other words, if they allow the truth of who they are, the lie immediately disintegrates, the illusion is exposed, and all immediately returns to its natural state of peace and love.

The reference in the story to their "nakedness" means that the lie is vulnerable to exposure. And thus the metaphor continues as they hide their bodies in "shame." The shame in this story refers to the fear of being exposed. A lie must always hide, so as not to be exposed. Once exposed, the lie loses its power and will therefore cease to exist. The shame also means that they have "dis-graced themselves." They no longer live in a state of grace.

At this point, Adam and Eve attempt to hide from God. They are now into the full force of their illusion, and they believe that such a thing is possible. They are now in a full-fledged state of false identity or ego. What is the nature of this false identity? Quite simply, it exists at its origin as a statement called "I am *not* God." This, by the way, is where the concept of "original sin" came from. *Sin* is easily defined as that which goes against God. Original sin refers to the very first time this happened. So original sin refers to the very first act that plunged humankind into a finite world of existence. The reason it is said by some that all of humanity is born with this original sin is because all of humanity continues to exist in the result of this original act. They are born again and again into this finite, physical Earth.

Here it is important to be clear about one thing. The story of Adam and Eve is a metaphor about what happens when the original lie enters the creative principle. It is not to be misconstrued as a story implying guilt about human beings. After all, the manifestation of this lie exists throughout your Universe! The story is simply told from a human perspective since that was the main focus of those who authored the story.

Adam and Eve find themselves unable to remain in the beautiful kingdom of Infinite Love. They find themselves "banished," and they realize that they are unable to coexist with God in the Infinite Universe. Because they now see God as separate, and therefore threatening, in their illusion, they see God as banishing them. They are no longer able to see truth in their new experience of good and evil. God is now "punishing" them, or so they believe. Everything they see is now an illusion.

Here is how they interpret their plight. They believe that God is now telling them things in their delusional state of so-called separation.

Now that they are in this delusional state, something is always right or wrong, good or bad. In the case of their denial, God is seen as a threatening force who is judging them as good or bad. They see God as the proverbial dictator who threatens them and controls their lives.

The truth of the matter is that by absorbing the original lie, this creative force of man and woman, yin and yang, or whatever you want to call it, produces a new set of physics, all of which are illusionary in nature. Now we have violence, death, pain, suffering, and everything else that goes along with existing in a finite world. The story suggests that humankind will no longer exist in the Garden of Eden, the Infinite world of Love, and will be banished into the finite where they will struggle and toil as they attempt to survive on their own in their now manifesting illusion that they are *not* God. Is this starting to make sense to you? Is this starting to sound familiar?

The story also suggests that humankind will be relegated to a world of reproduction, birth, and death. Why? Because it is impossible to sustain oneself indefinitely in a state called "I am *not* infinite. I am *not* God." And thus ensues the ancient, endless saga of reincarnation, as souls seek to continue their existence in whatever temporary form they can. Now I assume, of course, that this last statement will be seen by some as highly offensive in nature since the ultimate offense that one can commit in this finite world of things is to question the existence of death. Is it really that threatening to you to question the existence of something that you already do everything in your power to avoid? Your heart tells you every day that life is precious and that you want to live, does it not?

So the story is not yet over, my dearest friends. You are living this story in your lives right now. What I am going to suggest to you is something that you may not have contemplated. If you can relate to this metaphorical example of what has occurred in your world of things, then why not envision a true and beautiful end to this finite story of mass illusion? And what might that end look like? Well, I will tell you this much. You cannot imagine the profound beauty of what awaits you after you awaken from this deep, unconscious slumber. Indeed, the lion *shall* lay down with the lamb as they did for eons before this first, original lie took hold in your Universe. There will be no such thing as vegetarianism because life shall not devour life in order to survive. Can you pray for this, dear friends? It is not as outlandish as you may think. It is the state that you always lived in before this plunge into the finite realm of lies and illusion.

No one is guilty in this saga of death and destruction. Remember that guilt is merely an excuse, and indeed another lie, to convince you that you must stay in your current, collective condition. Do not perceive yourself as guilty simply because you haven't been able to see your way out of this. That's what prayer is for. There is more help in this Universe than you could ever imagine! But the response is only as large as the prayer itself. If prayer is issued from an erroneous position, one that seeks to protect and verify the validity and necessity of this dual reality of so-called good and evil, then the only possible response shall be limited indeed by the nature of the prayer itself. Put another way, if you remain intent upon rationalizing and excusing the existence of this illusion called good and evil, life and death, etc., then the message that you send to the Universe is that you wish to keep things in this state of affairs.

CHAPTER 13

Transhumanism

Have you noticed the exponential growth of technology in your world? Perhaps you are happy with your iPods, iPads, and screens of every make and manufacture. And yet these things are soon to become obsolete as well. The next phase is to begin to install them into your head and other body parts. Perhaps you believe that this is all "new" technology. In fact, it is as "old as the hills," as the saying goes. I would suggest instead that it is as old as the stars themselves.

Now what do I mean by that? Let us first begin with the recognition that you upon this Earth tend to view everything as though it has never happened before anywhere in this Universe. I highly recommend that you step back for a moment and remember to witness the relative size of this planet in space. How tiny are you, after all? In fact, if you step back far enough—as your high-tech telescopes have done many times over—you would be hard pressed to even find this planet Earth at all!

Fortunately, size in no way indicates level of importance. All exists with equal value within the bosom of Infinite Love.

Let me say first that this Universe is teeming with life. You are not only part of the physical Universe, as you know it, but you are also part of an inter-dimensional reality. This brings us to a very interesting point, indeed. Before we get to that point, however, let us stand back in the world of time and space and observe a few things in your planetary history. The human development of technology goes back very far in time. No one here knows for certain when it started, but needless to say, multiple theories abound. The important thing to realize is that it is all fundamentally a product of the mathematical nature of the human brain. The human brain is a highly programmable, biological system. It is built upon a program to learn and to calculate at its most foundational level. It is programmed through its DNA to operate, protect, and heal the entire biological system at all times. Its ability to calculate is almost unfathomable to what is referred to as the conscious mind.

You, as a species, are very accustomed to considering yourselves to be part of an ecosystem on the physical, planetary level. You basically include in your perception of that ecosystem any and all things that you are capable of experiencing through your five physical senses. Now that you have basically mapped out the entire Earth, you find it relatively easy to perceive such an ecosystem on a global scale.

What you have failed to factor in, however, is that you are part of a wider, evolutionary ecosystem that you cannot see. But you have many clues as to its existence. The first clue is this: where did human beings derive the knowledge and inspiration to advance technology from a highly primitive state, say about ten thousand years ago, to the point where it is today? And why is that advancement occurring now at an ever-increasing hyper-speed? In the past hundred years, the growth of technology has exploded at exponential levels.

Are you witnessing the birth of a new life form in this Universe? Some would say yes. You don't really know how life gets created or how it evolves. You *think* you know, to be sure. But the fact is that you don't. How can I be so certain of this? Well, reason it out for yourselves. You base all of your knowledge on that which you already know. This causes a condition known as producing your own brand of completely closed logic—a closed, self-reinforcing system of logic that exists by virtue of denial of all that exists outside of it. Now to be sure, your species strives to expand the platform upon which that system of logic is built, but it is a very slow process because there exists an inherent mandate to continue to preserve the system as a whole. It is what can be referred to as maintaining sanity in your world, to put it in simple terms.

But there are times when the pressure to expand your logic platform outweighs the need to preserve it, and a quantum shift in perception suddenly occurs. It is much like a mental earthquake, if you will. In terms of creative capability, it is akin to shifting the gears in a car to a higher level of velocity in order to accommodate greater levels of speed.

But what is the driving force behind all of this creative capability? It is overly simplistic to say that it is merely God (as you understand God in your finite world). There will come a time in your future where such ideas will be considered the quaint meanderings of a relatively primitive species. A species that was only able to account for the immediate knowledge of its surroundings while having little or no idea about that which it did not know. What is important for you to take into consideration now is the fact that there are many other ecosystems at work in your world, none of which you are aware of on a collective level, primarily because they do not exist in your physical dimension of time and space. So if your belief is that you live in a vast void of a Universe, alone as it were, and that the only thing between you and that void is what you refer to as God, then you are missing some highly important understandings indeed.

You are essentially programmed to recognize data and various sensory perceptions within a certain range or vibrational frequency level. You would refer to it as your "dimension" of existence. In truth, there is no such thing as a dimensional reality. That is simply your way of conceptualizing that which you do not fully understand. The closest way to describe this in English (or any other Earth language of conception) would be to suggest that your DNA is turned on at certain frequency levels, so as to produce a certain, limited experience of reality. Believe it or not, your DNA can be easily manipulated from a wider version of reality to enable you at any point in time to see things in an entirely new way. Basically, I am saying that you are not alone in your creations.

Now this may alarm some of you—if you are very fond of thinking that every good idea comes from you alone. This is simply not the case. There is a vast quantum Universe all around you, much of which does not even exist in time and space as you know it. "So where is my independence?" you might ask. There is absolutely a level of independent experience, which is precisely why this overall communication is coming to you now. You do have the power to influence your overall reality. The real issue is seated in whether or not you are experiencing an accurate perception of that reality and its source.

So let us start at the beginning in terms of explaining a few fundamental truths. Who you are as a being exists as a perfect extension of Omnipresence, Love, and the Divine. It is indeed what you refer to as God, or Infinite Love. That is the baseline truth of all that exists in what I previously referred to as the Real World. All is a manifestation of God/Love. The issue for you now is that you no longer exist, in terms of your experience, in that Real World. Part of this was explained to you in my metaphorical interpretation of the Garden of Eden. But that does not mean that all is lost. Why? Because you still maintain a conscious awareness of your very beautiful heart.

Your heart is your only link to the Real World of the Divine. Now many misconstrue as the Real World to be the place where people go after they die. It isn't. As I said before, the so-called afterlife is very closely linked to the physical world in which you live. They are both equally as unreal. Now this may be hard for some people to accept because it all *feels* so very real, doesn't it? Let us distinguish what is actually real from what isn't. Again, your heart is the only true reality because it is that which links you inextricably and forever to that which is real. Your heart exists as an infinite source of divine Love because it is the point at which you were meant to manifest as an extension of the Divine.

Consider this for a moment. If your heart exists to manifest evidence of the Divine in the Universe and beyond, what then happens when you find yourself existing in a finite Universe? Can the finite truly conduct that which is termed Infinite? No, of course not. But you will see evidence of that beautiful energy of divine love in the actions of those on this planet who are in touch with their hearts and allow its vast inspiration of divinity to touch the hearts and minds of everyone else. So, yes, the divine can indeed motivate beautiful action on the part of anyone who lives in resonance with his or her true heart of hearts. And this is what is ultimately your true link to Reality.

What we must discuss now is the very real fact that this heartfelt connection may be in jeopardy due to the massive evolutionary event unfolding on planet Earth at this time.

What is Transhumanism? It is the place at which this massive evolutionary event touches the human species directly. But in order to understand that, we must first observe this change as it exists on a planetary scale. One of the greatest misperceptions that exists on this planet has to do with the issue of environmental destruction. Let me offer you a rather different approach. You are all no doubt familiar with the grave destruction of your trees and forests. Which, by the way, is absolutely a real cause of so-called climate change! But sadly, that is just a small part of this picture. There is currently unfolding what we would call a mass extinction of biological, planetary life. Your human species is a part of that extinction as you will note the increasing difficulty that humans are having in the simple act of reproduction. But let us focus for now on the other biological life forms of plants, animals, marine life, and insects. All species everywhere are being affected as their existence is being systematically displaced by something else. The weather is indeed changing. You no longer experience a global climate produced solely by elements and species that are native to biological life and therefore integrate with it. The gaseous content of your atmosphere is changing dramatically.

Now the currently favored viewpoint is to blame humanity for all of this, which of course, is easy to do because humans are so accustomed to feeling guilt. Naturally, in your current perception of total isolation in this Universe, who else could possibly be responsible? Let us change the story from "who" to "what." Let us step back and make a clear and totally neutral observation of the overall situation. If we take the human element out of this picture temporarily, for purposes of observation, we can see much more clearly because we are no longer filtering information through the lens of human guilt. Human guilt is thousands of years old. It is deeply encoded in your DNA, but you can no longer afford to assign credibility to that experience of guilt because it will ultimately be your undoing!

So now we can step back and view the planetary situation through a very *clean* pair of glasses because we have removed the ancient, encrusted film of very old human guilt. Now doesn't that feel just a little bit refreshing? So what do we see through this very clean pair of glasses? Let us engage the flexible power of thought for a moment and decide to picture this beautiful Earth prior to any technology. The only thing existing here are the natural elements and biological life. Can you see the Earth's aura? How strong is it? Pretty radiant, wouldn't you say? Do you see the planet's vibrant state of health in all of its natural systems? Do you sense the harmonious integration of all biological life? Do you see weather patterns that over the long-term ebb and flow naturally with the influences of the sun and its solar activity? Do you sense a powerful simplicity in the living integration of all the planet's natural energies?

This is Earth in its natural state. A vibrant garden of radiant beauty, natural bounty, and it is literally teeming with life. A beautiful blue jewel in space. Precious beyond belief!

So what do we have now? Let us look at Earth in its present condition. First, take a look at the aura of your planet. How vibrant is its life force overall? Do you sense biological imbalances? How about energetic imbalances? Rather than trying to verbally describe it all, a more effective approach is to simply look and feel. What has changed from the time of our first observation?

Now allow yourself to zoom in on technology. How much of it is currently present? Machines are literally everywhere. Humans are the caretakers and manufacturers of these machines, but this state of affairs is in reality changing right before your eyes. The machines will at some point become self-replicating and able to run and control themselves. They will become self-repairing and do a far better job of this than biological life. They will at some point begin to evolve by their own hands. Just like you do right now. The only difference will be that machines will not be dealing with something called death—a current factor of all biological life. They will learn to extract energy from the surrounding atmosphere. They will function with an endless source of power as they learn to tap into the very fabric of matter itself. At the current time, you do not have words assigned to such matters, but you will eventually, as your current vocabulary will necessarily need to expand. The machines, of course, will be smarter than your biological brain, which will necessitate dramatic augmentation of the human species, that is if you are still around in any sort of recognizable form.

Now here is the rub in all of this. There are those who are no doubt saying, "Well, I won't have to worry about any of this because by then I will surely be dead." How many of you believe in past lives? If so, did it ever occur to you that the life you are living right now will also be added to your stack of previous past lives? In other words, it is wise to assume that the life you are living right now is in reality a *past* life when viewed from somewhere else. With that being the case, where are you as you view *this* lifetime, *this* moment as a past experience?

One of the most dangerous positions that any human being can take, especially at this point in time, is that death is merely a convenient escape from pressing matters that you don't know how to deal with. This perspective will make you lazy on an evolutionary scale, and with the way things are going on your planet right now, no one can afford this seeming luxury. We strongly suggest that you immediately remove yourself from the spectrum of so-called aging and death in terms of the context in which you see yourself. No one ever dies. The body learns to disintegrate due to the physical factor of entropy and the encoded decomposition that exists in your biological DNA. But *you* cannot die. Period. Thus, you have a seriously vested interest in what happens here, particularly if you plan to return in another form. You are most likely to do this in order to continue to try to grow, learn, and resolve your previous unresolved issues from other lifetimes.

The only problem with this nifty little scenario of returning again and again is that things are changing dramatically, and you will no longer be able to count on returning to the same biological circumstances. In fact, you could find yourself trapped in a reality where you literally cannot die! This is not in any way to be construed as immortality, my dearest friends. Far from it. On the contrary, we are talking about changes so vast that your current state of consciousness can barely comprehend it. The primary goal on this planet is physical immortality. *Immortal*, in this context, is not to be confused with the Infinite. It is much the same as the so-called unlimited Universe of fractals. Unlimited likewise does not mean infinite. It simply refers to a branch of mathematics that is currently out of your reach.

So physical immortality still occurs in the finite Universe because the very definition of physical is finite. A biological body, as it stands now, cannot accommodate this desire to live for millions of years, maybe even billions. I don't care how many billions of years you may think you want to live in outer space (because, believe me, this will in no way be limited to Earth), you have *absolutely* not solved this problem of no longer existing in the Real World of Infinite Love.

Transhumanism exists as the notion that all biological life, and humans in particular, will have to change and evolve in order to continue to participate in the new, synthetic ecosystem that is rapidly evolving on this planet. It is this synthetic ecosystem that is displacing the natural, biological world all over this planet. This is what you learn to recognize when you remove human guilt from the equation. You should understand that the onward evolution of this synthetic world cannot be stopped. Short of the complete destruction of the human power base, and all current sources of electrical power, nothing will stop this forward march of an entirely new species of life.

So why should this matter to you? Maybe you like all of this machinery after all. But that is not the point, dearest friends. You currently find yourselves in a very small evolutionary window of choice. The choice is not about stopping the advancement of this artificial kingdom. It is far too late for that. But you have many choices in terms of your own consciousness. The purpose of this communication is to let you know that your current paradigm and points of reference are fast becoming obsolete.

What does spirituality mean in a synthetic world? That is a question of paramount importance. Ironically, it is a question that does not need to concern you, if you are fully cognizant of what is going on.

CHAPTER 14

The Angelic Kingdom

There is a great deal of misconception about the subject of angels. Some of what I am about to say might seem confronting if you are wholly determined to hang on to the limitation of your current beliefs. But to some of you, it will cause you to rejoice enormously in the knowledge that things are not as limited as you may have previously thought.

Why do angels have wings? That is indeed the first question that we must address because that perception is many, many thousands of years old. It is not that it is wrong; it is just that it limits your overall connection to the angelic realm because it is a perception that tends to displace you in time and space from a realm of exceedingly dear friends.

First of all, it is important to understand that your mind is an interpreter. We are talking now about an aspect of the mind that is relatively neutral. This is not the part of the mind that interprets your

Earth-based experience. This is the part of the mind that is deeply connected to the spectrum of energetic reality within which you reside in the Universe. If you will recall for a moment the story of Adam and Eve that we discussed earlier, you will remember the part where they ate of the fruit of the tree of the knowledge of good and evil. You will remember how we stated that this was in reality, the fruit of the first, original lie called "I am *not* Omnipresence. I am *not* Infinite." This therefore produced a new set of physics that existed as a product of the illusion that they were now living in. This, in terms of creation, is what put them in the world of the finite.

Angels do not live in the finite Universe, but they are capable of reaching through the veil of illusion in order to help those who find themselves on the other side of that veil. It should also be known here that the so-called Afterlife exists on the same side of the veil that you do. Now I know that is not common knowledge because people on Earth tend to believe that the Afterlife is where God really exists. Might I remind you that God exists *everywhere*. There is no place where God is not. This is where people tend to get themselves very confused.

"But what about where there is evil? Surely, Archangel Michael, you can't be saying that God exists there!" Indeed, I would say, you are right! And that is precisely why it is abundantly clear, if you care to look, that evil is an illusion. It is precisely why there can be no such thing.

"But what about the fact that we actually experience it?" Of course you experience it, I would say, but that doesn't mean that that experience is *real*. And yes, dearest friends, I know that this experience feels *so* real that it exists as the most virtual of all virtual realities known to humankind. Even your physical body exists as a virtual reality if you want to get technical about it. Why do you think it is capable of experiencing pain? Pain is simply not possible where God is, and once again, I remind you that God is indeed everywhere. Dare I say that pain is just another illusion? Now here is where people can get a little bit crazy and start to defend their illusion.

Let me tell you a little bit about your dearest friend, Yeshua. Some of you refer to him as Jesus the Christ. Jesus was known to have performed many "miracles" of healing, correct? First, let us define a miracle. A miracle is any place where God shows up in your experience, which is completely out of the flow of where this finite illusion is going at any given time. For example, if you have sustained an exceedingly painful injury to your leg, the normal trajectory of that illusion is for the pain to worsen until some finite remedy is applied, which hopefully supports the body in going through its normal healing process in time and space.

A "miracle" would occur if an experience of God, and therefore Reality, suddenly appeared at some point in that finite trajectory. That experience is akin to a light turned on in the darkness, and that experience literally exposes the fact, experientially, that pain and damage to the body are an illusion that doesn't really exist. And thus the "miracle" occurs. The body is suddenly whole again, and the injury disappears like the mirage that it actually is.

Miracles are confusing to people because they do not occur in the space-time trajectory of the finite Universe. Therefore they are deemed "acts of God" that cannot be explained. The problem with deeming it an act of God is that it implies that God has made a decision to apply this so-called miracle at a certain coordinate in time and space. This immediately brings up the question of worthiness. We have already discussed human beings' penchant for guilt. So this erroneous perspective that God somehow made a temporary decision to bring relief to one person, under one circumstance, only makes people less predisposed to more and greater "miracles" as they proceed to remember all the ways in which they believe themselves to be unworthy of these benevolent acts of God. This perspective then proceeds to induce fear and only makes things worse in the long run.

So how indeed did Yeshua overcome all of this fear and produce dramatic healings in spite of it? Well, it was actually quite simple. It has to do with something called resonance. The most important thing to know is that Yeshua was (is) absolutely *clear* that this finite world is merely a dramatic illusion. He absolutely *knew* the truth that God is everywhere. He *knew* that truth, and he indeed *was* (and *is*) that truth. There was no separation. All he had to do was look at somebody and *see* that truth before him. Because his *knowing*, *seeing*, and literally *being* that truth was so powerful, his resonating field of consciousness and energy was so strong that this finite illusion of pain, suffering, and likewise, literally couldn't exist in his presence. He actually demonstrated, on planet Earth, the very real fact that these things are illusions that don't exist. So how is that for a tremendous service?

The crucifixion is another matter altogether. That incident is so gravely misunderstood that we will save that topic for another occasion. Don't you find it interesting that the religions of the world have chosen to completely *fixate* on the so-called death of the Christ as their central point of worship? If you don't believe this, you have only to observe the central symbol of Christianity, which is the cross or crucifix. The instrument of death! That's what we need to focus on, right? That resurrection stuff is just an afterthought. Very peculiar indeed. But this should provoke some deep contemplation on your part if you care to entertain this extremely bizarre fact!

So let us get back to the subject of the appearance of wings on angels. Because you currently reside in a finite dimension, your mind is wholly calibrated to finite interpretation. As I said earlier, angels do not reside in the finite. Your finite mind does not have a way to process this, but it applies wings to its interpretation in order to signify that angels are of a higher caliber of consciousness and energy than the lowly Earth-based perception. This does not mean that angel wings are bad. On the contrary, they are quite beautiful because of what they signify: a recognition that there is something more than this finite world of things. In fact, there are many people who believe in angels who will readily admit that "angels don't *really* have wings." But humanity loves to see these wings because they bring comfort, hope, and peace to those who observe them. So as long as you may need them, let them remain.

So what are angels? Simply put, angels are beings of love and light. They exist as messengers of God and the Infinite. This means that they can bring forth that reality toward human beings, and all who dwell upon this Earth, whenever they are needed. Angels are the living proof that you are not alone. Angels are what we will call agents of evolution. In order to understand what that means, we must first define evolution. For purposes of this discussion, let us define evolution in a more profound way than merely assuming it is related to any species acquiring a better ability to cope with living in the finite.

Evolution, as we will define it, refers to waking up from the dream. It means a return to a state of sanity, where there exists Truth and only Truth. The lie of "I am *not*" ceases to exist. All there is is God, Truth, and Infinite Love. Indeed, that is all there is right *now*. The problem is that you don't experience it. Why? Because of the physics produced by the quandary of "I am not." Those physics produce for you a world of good/bad, right/wrong, justified/unjustified, and hate/love. If you wonder how this is possible, you have only to observe how much you can create with a simple zero/one interface.

Angels exist as the potential interface between you and your Real World of knowing. We are bringing up the subject of angels here because we would like to offer you an opportunity to expand your understanding of what is possible with their assistance. We would like to provide you with an opportunity to deepen your relationship with them. Now some people don't believe that they have any relationship with angels. And here, too, the unworthiness factor tends to get in the way. But angels are your communication link with the Divine. This can take many forms. It can come in the form of true inspiration, where creative ideas and solutions can be offered to you in the form of a brilliant idea that suddenly occurs in your mind. Angels can influence circumstances in your favor, when doing so will bring you closer to God, and greater experiences of love and success, when that success is beneficial to you and others in your life. They can offer you comfort and security when you might feel hopeless and afraid. They continuously remind you that Love is the only reality. Why is this important? Because living in this finite kingdom of life can easily cause you to forget all of these things. The love of the Divine reaches out to you at all times in the comforting form of angels to remind you and help you stay connected to that which is the only true reality. Love and the Infinite.

Now because of all the filtering that goes on in this finite kingdom in which you currently reside, by the time the presence of angels passes through these multiple filters in your perception, they appear to you as exceedingly etheric. This is not an actual or accurate sensory perception of the true magnitude of their power and beauty, but by the time they have passed through all of your filters, they either can't be seen at all, or what can be seen is rather wispy in nature. This should never be construed as any sort of limited fact about their existence. Angels, in truth, are not etheric at all! In fact, it is actually *you* who is etheric. Now this will surely be a blow to your perceived idea about yourselves. Allow me to enlighten you about a few things.

Just because you are unable to pass your hand through a brick wall does not necessarily mean that you are solid, and therefore more real than your etheric perceptions of the Universe, and specifically angels. This appearance of your finite world being solid is the result of the physics produced by the "I am *not*" principle, where everything in the finite clashes with everything else. You know it as things being known by what they are *not* rather than by what they *are*. You kind of know yourself that way, don't you?

Start with the unfortunate experience of "I am *not* God." If a tree exists in the finite as "I am *not* the car," then when the moving car reaches the tree, the car and the tree will quickly let each other know that they are definitely *not* one another. You will know this for sure by the damage and destruction that they will thereby do to each other.

Everything in the finite is threatened by everything else, and that is a simple way to explain the physics of why you cannot put your hand through a wall without some real damage occurring. For any scientists out there who find this description to be wholly inadequate, I simply say, "Lighten up!" Your language is the real inadequacy here; it in no way accounts for that which you cannot understand, see, or experience.

Let us now discuss why angels can be so important to you now. Your world is currently spiraling into a state of greater and greater chaos. All of your previous belief systems are going to be more and more challenged. It will become increasingly difficult to maintain a sense of peace, serenity, and balance. Yet these things are absolutely necessary if you are to retain any sense of clarity at all. Thus angels are always here to help you find your way, if you should humbly ask for their assistance.

It should also be known that angels are always present to help and support all life while the Universe slowly rights itself from this grand illusion, and Truth is restored throughout.

It is not necessary to see or know of angels on a conscious level in order to receive their assistance. Many times they are helping you when you are not aware of it at all. Angels will always respond to a sincere heart. They always respond to love. They are beautiful companions in the cosmos who are unlimited in their ability to assist you, love you, and support you in finding your way back to your true home. They will help you through all of life's transitions in this finite experience, to be sure. They even assist you and accompany you and all of your loved ones at your multiple times of physical departure as you continue to wend your way through many lifetimes in the grand illusion produced in this finite Universe.

But we want you to know that you are now at a juncture that requires more. It is no longer enough for you to merely expect your beautiful angelic friends to help you to cope with this finite experience, for all the reasons expressed in the previous chapter. We ask you, for the sake of yourselves, to consider opening the doors of your perception wider and to be exceedingly true to your hearts. Allow the angels to help you learn to be uncompromising in your allegiance to your own heart. Your heart will light the way. Your angels will hold your hand and guide you. All you have to do is ask.

CHAPTER 15

The Ego

The subject of the ego is perhaps one of the most important things to understand if you are to achieve any level of mastery in this lifetime. In order to understand it, we must first discuss a few things about the nature of a human being. We will dispel a few myths along the way.

Let us begin with one of the most grave and erroneous assumptions that human beings have made about themselves. There exists a very prevalent mindset here that has been around for a very long time. "If it exists in a human being, then we must include it as part of the nature of what it means to be human." Now this is very tricky because when you take that sentence at face value, it sounds very scientific and intelligent, doesn't it? This statement is usually followed by "So, of course, since God created everything, everything that exists in this so-called human nature must have been created by God." And an additional follow-up statement claims, "Since good and evil both exist in humankind, then it means that God must have created human beings with both good and evil." Have you understood enough in reading so far to finally know why that statement is erroneous? Just a little test to see if you've been paying attention! But if not, don't worry. I am happy to explain.

It goes without saying that Love cannot beget hate. Likewise, Love cannot beget evil. So where do these things come from? Well, in truth, they don't come from anywhere because by definition, they exist as the absence of something. Let us go back to the beginning. If you say, "I am *not* Omnipresence," it is the same as saying, "I am *not* Infinite." It is likewise the same as saying, "I am *not* Love," since God is Infinite, Omnipresent Love.

"I am *not* Love" can only mean one thing: "I am therefore the *absence* of Love." Now think this through, dearest friends. Is there such a thing as the absence of anything, really? Or does the absence of anything really refer to nothing? If you say, "I am *not* there," are you there or are you completely *absent* from wherever there is? And if you are absent from wherever there is, can anyone find that you exist in that place? Of course not. It could be easily stated that you literally do not exist wherever *there* is. If someone insisted that your absence in that place was indeed a "presence" of some kind, you would clearly see that they were in some sort of an illusion to believe such a thing. Why? Because there is really nobody there! In its most graphic sense, you would have to say that it was a "lie" to say that your absence in that place was really a presence. That is how the illusion of the finite works. There is no such thing as *not* infinite because infinite means everywhere. How could there exist the *absence* of the infinite? Yet that is what the finite pretends to be. Thus, it exists as a massive illusion. (For those who think that the infinite has something to do with numbers, it doesn't. It refers to the omnipresent state of God, which is Love.)

The fact that you perceive yourself to be living in a non-infinite state puts you immediately into an illusion of separation from God, the Infinite Omnipresence of Love. Do you see how that works? This separation then begins to manifest at every level of consciousness as an irreconcilable duality. This duality begins with your erroneous perception that you are *not* God. The perception that you are *not* infinite is why you manifest a finite body for your infinite self. How's that for a major duality? Thus you struggle to reconcile the inherent knowledge that *you* don't feel any older, and *you* of course wish to keep on living forever, yet you look in the mirror and see this strange body of yours aging and eventually dying. What in the world is *that* all about? You wonder about it in amazement—until you finally feel forced to accept it. But it confuses you, does it not? What is the point in dying, anyway? You were just starting to get the hang of living on this planet! Why go now?

So let us focus on this inherent duality in order to understand the ego. This understanding *must* start with the full recognition that *you* are an infinite being. This is not philosophical conjecture. There is clear evidence to this fact that exists in your everyday experience. You do not relate to aging. You do not relate to dying. In fact, in your so-called youth, it is nearly impossible for you to imagine such things. You do not understand why you cannot eat anything you want, just for the fun of it. What is this unfamiliar thing of needing to take care of and preserve a body? You are more than happy to pretend that sleep is optional if there are other things that you'd rather be doing. Muscle atrophy? You mean I have to intentionally exercise in order to prevent it? These, my dear friends, are all concerns that do not exist in the Real World of Infinite Love, where all is sustained because it exists as what it is rather than what it isn't. You come here familiar with the infinite because it's who you are.

So now you find yourself here again with yet another Earth body, living in the finite. The only problem is that you have forgotten everything you learned the last time because you are basically starting all over again with a new body. So you rummage around in the darkness, trying to remember who you are and why you're here, for the umpteen millionth time.

Enter the ego to help you out! What exactly is the ego? It exists as an alternate identity whose role it is to help you navigate through the finite. The ego is the opposite of you because it completely understands and subscribes wholeheartedly to the finite world of illusion. There are people who say that the ego is vital and important because it is what provides a person with their sense of identity. Indeed, this is true. The only problem is that it is a *false* identity, which is made up mostly of who you're *not*. Have you ever noticed that the ego always speaks to you in dual terms? If you are good, it's because someone else is bad. If you are bad, it's because someone else is better than you. The ego always speaks in irreconcilable terms of differences and separation.

How does the ego get created? Again, we must observe the strange new laws of physics that are created by the first, original lie of "I am *not*." Remember that "I am not Infinite" produces an immediate illusion of the absence of God and the Real World. You, who are an infinite being, must find an alternate identity in order to know who you are in this finite world. That identity gets created automatically by default. It represents wherever the infinite *you* is absent in the finite world. It is the reason that there is so much confusion around the body. People identify themselves as being their bodies, and then they are shocked when something happens to it or when it physically perishes. They simply can't believe it. This confusion is the result of the dual reality that gets created when infinite consciousness attempts to live through the illusion of a finite body. This body is then piloted by a false identity to account for it all. So, no, you are definitely not crazy when you find yourself shocked at the so-called natural degradation of your physical, finite body. It is simply who you are—an infinite being of love who knows nothing about entropy, death, and destruction. The illusion will always shock you, no matter how many times you experience it.

Hopefully now you have some degree of clarity about the difference between *you* and this false illusion of the finite. And if you do, then perhaps you are ready to examine where you personally stand with this peculiar false identity known as the ego. Do you know about the voice in your head? Of course you do! It's the one that talks to you all day long, and sometimes all night long. It's like a little general, always barking orders and informing you about what's *really* going on. It is the great interpreter that substitutes for pure knowledge and consciousness. It eclipses clarity and creates confusion by casting doubt on everything that you would naturally be sure of. Think you want to pursue the profession of your dreams? The ego is happy to protect you from failure by letting you know what a failure you already are so you won't waste time trying, only to fail again! See how helpful it can be? It has just helped protect you from all that pain.

The ego creates enormous confusion because it produces an illusion that you have two identities. One is your true identity, which is that of your infinite self, and the other is what is known as your false identity, which is that of the ego. The true identity, which is centered in your heart, is one of peace, love, and creativity. It is one of hope and eternal inspiration. It exists as the seat of your true intelligence. It judges no one, and it never wishes ill upon anyone. It is completely secure in the knowledge of the Infinite God and Divine Love. It does not know fear.

The false identity, on the other hand, is that which is created to operate in the finite and ensure that you are well situated in all of its duality. It manipulates you through fear and judging others. It interprets every situation as one of haves and have-nots. It does not care if you are happy or miserable. Its only goal is to preserve itself. People are fond of saying, "Everyone has an ego—it's a part of life—and therefore we must learn to live with it." But it is vitally important to understand *why* it is there and for what purpose. Its purpose is to ensure your dedication to this finite illusion. That is why it always speaks in irreconcilable terms of good/bad, right/wrong, hate/love, and life/

death. These dualities can never be reconciled with one another, and thus you remain forever trapped in this finite illusion. The erroneous way that you have attempted to reconcile these dualities is primarily through religion and various brands of spirituality. Primarily, the gist is to say that God has ordained all of this for a very good reason, which is _____ (fill in the blank). In this case, "God" is not the God of Infinite Love. On the contrary, this "God" exists as the very same illusion that promoted the first, original lie. This "God" represents an allegiance to the finite.

Now many of you believe that the answer to this state of dual realities is to bring more love and light into this planetary sphere of existence. This is absolutely noble and helpful, but as you can see by the world around you, that is not nearly enough. Until the core principle that is creating all of this is directly addressed, the love that you bring in will be heavily resisted as a threat to that which you have termed the "darkness," which in reality is merely the absence of Truth. Again, the "I am *not*." Love is pure presence. I am *not* Love is an absence. This absence is created by the lie of *not*, or the resistance to that truth. This is why prayer and the angelic kingdom are so important to you now. The context of your prayer is vital. It can either be a context of supporting and excusing the death and destruction inherent in the finite world—in which case, you will continue to receive the help that you ask for in dealing with it as best you can—or the context of your prayer can be profoundly expanded. You can actually pray for the final elimination of the principle that sources this mass illusion of death and destruction. But in order to do that, you will have to sacrifice your notion of human guilt. Your consciousness will have to change to one of recognition of what is really going on in this Universe in order to pray the powerful prayers that you are truly capable of.

The ego does not want you to recognize this. The day that you do, its demise is imminent. It can only exist as a product of the lie of what you are *not*. It can never exist as the truth of what you *are*.

Now let me say something about the truth of that which is I, Archangel Michael. Allow me to offer you an example of the limited condition that your formerly small context of prayer has produced. If you pick up any published book informing you about the various natures and so-called specialties of your beloved guardian angels, you will no doubt find a passage about myself. "Archangel Michael is here to help you with your fears." This belief comes from a completely erroneous context that presumes that the whole Universe subscribes to your current rationale that you must learn to cope, adapt, and somehow overcome these obstacles in your lives. I am here to inform you that there is a far greater possibility than these, and until you entertain that possibility, you will continue to struggle and live in the darkness produced by this finite illusion.

Your angels are dear and powerful friends who have capabilities that can only be limited, in terms of their response, to the limitations of your requests for help. As long as the entire world refuses to take seriously what Yeshua and others like him proved to you beyond any shadow of a doubt, you will continue to pray prayers of weakness and guilt. The results of those prayers can only match the magnitude of the prayers themselves. Why? Because as you well know, you are the one who ultimately determines your destiny, collectively and individually. That destiny is determined by your heart. If your allegiance remains with the ego instead, you will remain frustrated, confused, and unable to surrender to Love. The ego will always present you with the dualities of good/bad, right/wrong. That is a trap that has no door. As long as you continue to follow it, you can never get out.

What we are proposing to you is the possibility that you can listen to the truth that your heart holds within. In so doing, you can lift your head above the smoke and mirrors of the ego and finally experience the tremendous power and peace afforded you by clarity and oneness of perception. You do not have to buy into the false duality that the ego presents you with every day, every moment. We strongly encourage you to consider this possibility, perhaps for the first time ever.

Your heart and you are one and the same. Your heart can only want Love because it *is* Love. So this is not a matter of coming up with something new. It is a matter of what you are allied with. The ego exists as a manifestation of the source of fear. Pay attention to how much it tries to intimidate either yourself or others. Pay attention to the fact that it will happily "crucify" you or someone else. It doesn't care about pain or suffering. It doesn't care if it keeps you up all night, telling you how hopeless things are or how royally you messed things up. It is more than happy to intimidate you into self-repression, out of a fear of not being good enough. On the other hand, it is happy to repeatedly manifest for you the famous saying: *pride goes before a fall*. It will set you up for that again and again, if you let it.

And why, after all, do you need a voice in your head instead of pure consciousness and knowing? It is because the ego exists as *not* you, and it must therefore remind you of its existence on a wholly perpetual basis.

CHAPTER 16

The Purpose of Life

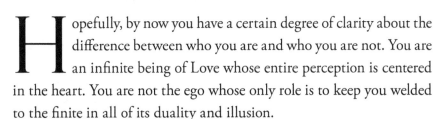

Hopefully, by now you have a certain degree of clarity about the difference between who you are and who you are not. You are an infinite being of Love whose entire perception is centered in the heart. You are not the ego whose only role is to keep you welded to the finite in all of its duality and illusion.

The point to be made right now is that you come here, to this planet, to this reality, with a purpose. Perhaps you thought that this purpose was entirely limited to your so-called life span, which if it were to match the usual term, would only last for about one hundred years. Since the body would begin to deteriorate long before that, if that is the only context you can muster, you have about as much time as an ant, relatively speaking, when it comes to your true capability and intelligence. This ever-so-short term of life affords you almost no chance at all to do anything of much significance, unless you are highly unusual and clear. And even for those who manage to make a seriously significant contribution, there is still never enough time.

So what does one do? The first thing is to greatly enlarge the span and scope of your context, starting again with the recognition that you are an infinite being. Your infiniteness needs to become primary, instead of some secondary, philosophical reality that you keep in the closet 99 percent of the time. Except, of course, when you are meditating and there is no necessity of a physical manifestation or outward expression of that reality. Meditation is indeed important because it gives you a chance to be with *you*—without any of the distractions of the outside world. Of course, the ego will be there to make sure you don't get *too* far into it and accidentally lose track of who you're *not*! That's why meditation can be so difficult for so many people. They simply don't know what to do about the annoying voice in the head that continuously distracts them with every irrelevant thought and idea that it can possibly muster. Do you know that you actually don't have to put up with that annoying little voice? Try it sometime. Decide to be in command of your consciousness, and simply refuse to entertain it.

So what does it mean to orient your entire existence in the fact that you are infinite? It means an instant recognition that you are *already* beyond birth and so-called death. You are consciously larger than those two events and whatever time spans between them. This experience is of paramount importance if you are to expand your options of life's purpose and how you understand that opportunity. Otherwise, there is a good chance that you will fall prey to the ego's interpretation of your life's purpose. The ego has a wild assortment of crazy ideas about the purpose of anyone's life. Here are a few examples, but believe me, there are many more!

For example, the ego will often come up with the idea that no matter what you do, the goal should be to be better than anyone else. This, of course, will necessitate a perpetual state of judging yourself against the successes and failures of other people around you. One of the ego's favorite games has to do with sports. That arena of entertainment provides a veritable feast for the egos of the world. There are only so many people who can actually play sports at a professional level, but the ego is not to be daunted as long as judgment is around! It can get millions and millions of people to sit at home and yell at their TV sets in full-fledged judgment of how well or poorly those athletes are doing. The ego will always tell these people that they, of course, are *way* smarter and *way* better than those physical athletes on the field. It will never fail to remind these imaginary sofa athletes that if they were on that field, that *of course* they would all perform like supermen and superwomen! They would never make a mistake. They would always score *big*! They know *way* better how the game is played, and they are not afraid to let their TV sets know it!

If you find this amusing, you might want to take a look at how prevalent this behavior is in everyday life. It literally exists everywhere. How about all those drivers on the road, cursing the bad driving of everyone else? Imagine how much yelling and cursing is really going on inside all those cars in rush-hour traffic. How many people drive through their own neighborhoods listening to the ego tell them how good or bad their neighbors' upkeep of their houses are? And all the while the ego is letting that same driver know how well he or she measures up to those neighbors.

One of the ego's definite favorites exists in the realm of childrearing. It's like a contest, isn't it? Whose child is the most successful? The ego always enjoys pitting parents against one another in competition for whose child is at the top of any proverbial ladder. It even exists in the realm of spirituality. Who is on top of the spiritual totem pole in any spiritual organization? And, of course, the most famous one is all about money. Who has the most? Who has the least? And what does it all mean? It's a good thing the ego does not have a physical voice; otherwise, it would suffer from chronic laryngitis from all this yelling and judging of everyone else.

Why is this important in terms of life purpose? Because in the ego's ever-present habit of multitasking as it constantly informs you about literally every issue in your life, it can become very difficult to achieve true clarity in the form of listening to your heart. Because the ego is founded in fear, it uses fear to manipulate you into doing whatever it wants you to do. If it wants you to keep your head low, fit in, and not make waves, that's easy to accomplish with a little dose of intimidation and low self-esteem. If it wants you to be noticed and praised by others, it can also use fear of rejection to send you off in that direction. Its tricks and manipulations are virtually endless.

But what does any of this have to do with your heart? What does any of this have to do with true inspiration? Well, nothing, of course! The heart is not about fear; it's about love. The heart, in truth, is about your infinite self. The ego is about your finite self. Fear is its only motivation because in the finite world of things, the most important thing is to survive. Now you cannot have two selves. One of them has to be false. Which one do you think it is?

Up until present times in this so-called modern age, the social-political conditions were relatively predictable. Even before that, it was always predictable that this was a planet of biological life. So you could pretty much adhere to the basic philosophy that life was about coming here and doing the best you could under the circumstances. If it was a time of war, you coped with that. If it was a time of peace in your part of the world, you dealt with your options accordingly. But it was pretty much a given that you would find yourself in a biological body (human or otherwise, depending upon your beliefs), living among humans who were basically doing the same thing. You would eventually grow old, if you were lucky, and then pass on into another dimension where you would have the opportunity to assess how well you did before moving on to something else.

While you were here, it could all be a rather ho-hum situation where it didn't *really* matter how things turned out in the long run because the consequences could be addressed whenever and however you wished. (Do you find yourself living that way today, by any chance?) You see, the ego will always tell you that it's okay. The ego will tell you that it doesn't *really* matter when you get around to anything because you have *plenty* of time! It will even tell you this for fifty or sixty years—no problem! Then it will suddenly say, "You know what? You're too old! You can't do anything now!"

But all of this evolutionary malaise will soon be coming to a close, as a brand-new life form begins to emerge on planet Earth. Now brand-new does not necessarily mean desirable. If all goes as planned, there will come a point in the future where you will not even recognize this place. As I said in the beginning of this discourse, planet Earth is being rapidly transformed into a vastly different kind of place. You can already see her beauty wearing thin. This is the subject that we must address if you wish to be proactive for the Earth and for your own evolution as a being.

At some point, there is a good chance that machines will become self-aware. You should know that that is the plan. Do you think that this is impossible? Well, it is no more impossible than biological life being self-aware. Machines will have a greater advantage in this finite Universe. They can be programmed to have absolutely no awareness of the infinite, even if they themselves are self-aware. That pesky heart would no longer be a problem.

"So what, Archangel Michael? Machines already have no connection to the infinite; what does that have to do with us humans?" You are forgetting one thing, my dearest friends. You are forgetting about human augmentation. At some point in the future, the plan is to merge human beings with machines. This effort is already well under way, and most people are very happy to participate as they enjoy the modern conveniences of smartphones and the like. You can reason this out for yourself as you witness more and more of your collective consciousness being embedded inside of computers.

Can you stop this process? It is highly doubtful. You may have already noted that it is nearly impossible to communicate effectively without the use of a computer.

So what is the point? It is still a finite Universe. In that regard, nothing has really changed, you might say. Well, that is true, except for one thing. With the advent of the machine world, it will become increasingly difficult to connect with your own heart—unless you proactively deal with that situation right now. The infinite heart is soon to become just another part of the scientific world, and it will all be explained away as being mathematically represented along with everything else. Consciousness will be seen as something that can be embedded anywhere, as humans proceed to attempt to download themselves into a virtual world of anything goes. Love will be interpreted as a mere chemical reaction that can be easily duplicated artificially. Even so-called spiritual experiences will be artificially created in laboratory settings, thereby invalidating anything resembling the real thing. This will all sound wonderful and free to many, mostly because the level of evolutionary laziness will have reached an all-time high, and the prospect of having all these experiences, virtual though they may be, will become irresistible. Imagine all that fun and artificial joy for free—with no effort at all! Just a program.

Can you guess what the problem is with all of these wondrous ideas? You will still remain an Infinite being of Love. But in what avenue will you be able to find an experience and expression of that truth? And what will be the consequences to your soul?

This is a very big Universe. Time, as you understand it, means nothing. Trillions of Earth years would only exist as a blip. There is a virtually unlimited amount of space in which the finite can continue to manifest. Believe me, you have not even begun to see all the ways in which this can happen. But lest you become overwhelmed, let me help you to keep this simple. You have only to focus on your own experience and make every effort to preserve the experience of your infinite, beautiful heart. The sincerity in that heart is like gold. It is what connects you to God and the Truth of Divine Love. Nothing can remove that from you. Nothing. You are always secure in that experience, but it is vital that you nurture and cultivate that experience in yourself and others. Consider it precious, beyond all else.

Let us now get more specific about the nature of knowing your individual life's purpose. This is a gigantic and often frustrating puzzle for many, isn't it? What should I do with my life? The main problem that most of you have with ascertaining this is that you tend to put it in the category of having a job. Now you may have a perfectly good job already. If that is the case, you will find yourself thinking along the lines of a life purpose that competes with your job. You are likely to choose the job and toss out the life's purpose simply because the job provides you with your necessary financial security. Or you could take the opposite road, quit your job, and then assume that miracles will happen and in some mysterious way, your financial life will remain intact. Those who have tried that road have generally found that this approach doesn't work too well. Once the job is gone, and the money along with it, they find themselves scrambling in desperate fear to find a way to survive. This is not exactly the best environment of consciousness in which to serve humanity, is it?

Our first suggestion is to not put this issue in the category of a job. That way, you can truly relax about it and be more in touch with yourself. The most important thing that you can do is to find the time *outside* of your current employment in which to contemplate and then act upon your true desire to have a meaningful purpose. Try turning off the TV. Step away from the Internet. Free yourself up in ways that do not threaten your current livelihood. Take time out in nature to get a feel for your natural relationship to the Earth. The heart is like a beautiful plant. It needs to be tended and nurtured if you want to experience it in a world that has little or no use for it.

Here are a few hints to help you know where to look when trying to discover your individual purpose in life. A lightworker is essentially a person who deeply cares about the Earth. It is someone who feels a general affinity for the natural world and feels drawn toward experiences of peace, love, fairness, and tranquility. When given a choice between love and hate, they will always seek the light of love, even if they have patterns of behavior that would urge them otherwise. Lightworker is a very loosely defined term simply because it is so broad. There are many people on this Earth who do not even know of this term, yet it absolutely applies to them. It is not a title or a destiny. It is simply a way to identify those who truly care about the outcome of this planet and their own lives.

Lightworkers are essentially people who bring the light of love and positivity into the surrounding space and to people they meet. They are generally sincere, even though their lives may be difficult. They may be artists, healers, spiritual teachers, mothers, fathers, lovers, and friends. They may even work in professions that appear to have no spiritual causes whatsoever. They are often angels in human form. They are simply people who love and care.

Lightworkers are not perfect. They may have many challenges, personal and otherwise, but what sets them apart is sincerity and a willingness to try.

Being a lightworker is not a label. It is not even a profession. It is solely a matter of the heart. People, animals, plants, and pretty much all living things who seek the light of love depend upon the grace and goodness of lightworkers. Many times, they function as an extension of angelic grace, even though they might be totally unaware that this is their role. It doesn't matter because all is united as one beautiful force in Love.

Right now, the Earth is in great need on every single level. The overall despair is palpable. If you have read this far, then consider that the time has come to surrender your guilt. Your guilt is the thing that stands in the way of you essentially manifesting the core of who you really are on this planetary sphere called Earth. Your ego will tell you that you are guilty of many things, and that that is why you should slink away with your proverbial tail between your legs, letting someone else fulfill the role of contribution. This is a simple trick, and you do not have to fall for it. You do not have to tolerate a voice inside your head, posing as "you," telling you that you are guilty of being a failure, a loser, incompetent, hopeless, or otherwise. God is none of these things, and it is impossible for them to be real.

Even if the ego can produce a massive backlog of evidence for why its harsh judgment of you and your life is so justifiably negative, you might remind yourself that the reason that all of this evidence may exist in the first place is because of the very existence of the ego itself. It doesn't matter whether that ego was in you, or in someone else who harmed you. What is the thing that all of this time has been telling you how terrible it all is? What is it that told you there was no hope? What is it that provided only fear and absolutely no love in your darkest hour? Is this really the thing you want to listen to?

CHAPTER 17

The Body

Let us begin by taking a radical new view of the body. This, of course, starts with context. Let me first describe for you the usual context of the body on planet Earth. The body is essentially owned by the ego. How do you know this? Because for the majority of people, the belief is that they *are* their bodies. After all that we have discussed so far, do you think that that is really possible? Of course not. Do you remember that you have only *one* identity, not two? You are an infinite being of light and love. Period. There is nothing else. The body is a finite manifestation. Because you are not finite, a substitute identity takes over that is equally as finite so that you can be functional in the finite world. This false identity, or ego, literally supplants your true consciousness wherever it can. In the same way that the finite body always deals with matters inherent in the physics of the finite, so too does the ego present all of life as being about the same duality.

The first duality exists in the separation between you and your body. If the truth be told, you should never be occupying a finite body. It makes no sense, does it? True nature would never create such a discrepancy. An infinite being would of course exist in an equally infinite body. That is what the Real World is all about. Now there is no such thing as a finite body. That is where the illusion lies. I have no doubt that this is exceedingly difficult, if not impossible, to grasp in your current situation. That is all right. For now, try to remember what I said earlier about your dearest friend, Yeshua. Perhaps that will give you a tiny clue.

In fact, in the Real World, there is no such thing as "occupying" a body at all! You and your body are one and the same. There is no division. It is all one. Now for those of you who think that "channeling" is weird, it is! Are you surprised? Well, don't be. Reason it out for yourselves. What is weird is a world that is so detached from the Truth, in terms of the Real World of Infinite life, love, and God itself, that unless beings are willing to incarnate in this situation, they cannot be seen, heard, or recognized. The only problem is that if they do incarnate, their pure essence is so eclipsed by the finite that it is exceedingly difficult, if not impossible, to manifest and express their purest, most expansive self.

We have long maintained that this language—and all Earth-based languages—is absolutely inadequate for communicating most of what you really need to know. Why is that? Because the languages of this planet are all about what is already known. And even worse, they are only there to describe a finite experience of virtually everything. Our communication is primarily energetic, and it occurs mostly on unseen levels. The words are here merely to get your attention. As far as the subject of channeling goes, it is sometimes the most expedited way to bring forth communication on a conscious level, where someone such as myself can be seen and/or heard. This will never be optimal, however. What is truly optimal is for all of *you* to rejoin the Real World of Infinite life, where such things as channeling don't exist. But in the meantime, let us take advantage of the fact that there are some ways that we can connect now, in this far-from-optimal situation.

In the same way that channeling is strange, it is equally as strange for you to be separate from your own body. If this confuses you, reflect back for a moment about what I said earlier when I described the fact that you, yourself, don't relate to aging. You certainly don't relate to dying. Think about all of the ways in which you are surprised at all the trials and tribulations that your physical body goes through in any given lifetime. Think about how shocked and surprised you are any time that you or a loved one experiences an injury. This stuff continues to feel unfamiliar to you—no matter how many times you experience it. These things will simply *never* be familiar to an infinite being. What about plastic surgery? This is simply a way to try to force the finite body to more closely represent what you think would be a more adequate and timeless expression of yourself. But it is highly primitive indeed! Why do human beings dye their hair when they reach a certain age? Because they are trying to get the body to match what they know in their hearts is a truly ageless state of affairs. Eventually, people tend to give up as the body succumbs to the physics of the finite and deteriorates past all points of repair.

And how does the ego view all of this? Well, the ego thinks this is all just fine! Anything that has a beginning and an end is absolutely great as far as the ego is concerned. The more deterioration, the better! The ego likes the fact that your life has a definite beginning and a definite ending. It's marked by those numbers on every tombstone. It proves to the ego that life is most definitely a finite affair. Why is this important? Because in the finite, it's all about defined lines and survival.

The only way the ego can recognize you is by what *isn't* you. The time before birth, when the body wasn't, and the time after death, when the body won't be, provide the perfect lines of delineation that the ego requires to identify you as a "thing" with clear boundaries in time and space. The ego simply cannot recognize the infinite. This is also why the entire finite Universe can be defined in mathematical terminologies. It's all about definite numbers. But you should know that no matter how unlimited any amount of numbers may seem, those numbers in no way equate the Infinite. The Infinite is not the sum of the parts; I don't care how many parts there are. If there are too many for you to count, or even comprehend, it does not change the fact that this is still a very finite situation. Even if you discover that these numbers eventually roll over into a brand-new dimension of mathematics, and even if you discover that these rollovers can go on indefinitely, you are still dealing with the underpinnings of the finite world.

So let's talk for a moment about death. People like to marvel at how much of life is so-called wasted. What do they mean by this? They mean that everyone should remain fully cognizant of the fact that they are eventually going to die. What do you think birthdays are about after all? They are there to remind you, in case you forgot, that you likely have only so many years left to live. Birthdays are a way to emphasize and celebrate the fact that you live in a finite reality. Birthdays are all about math, aren't they? Let's count how many times the Earth has traveled around the sun since the day you were born. Then let's look at the average number of orbits that human beings in your part of the world tend to experience before they depart. Now subtract the first number from the second. Voila! You always know where you are in that finite spectrum of life.

Death also breeds tremendous unconsciousness. Life becomes more about fitting in as much stuff as possible in a very limited amount of time, while you still can. This is the equivalent of shopping at a sale and trying to get as much as you can for the smallest amount of money. How many items can you squeeze in for a certain dollar amount? How many things can you try to experience in a limited number of years? A good deal would be to get as many years as you can—with as much stuff in them as possible. It really is the same kind of math.

This may not be the most pleasant thing to contemplate, which is why unconsciousness is such a useful thing to have. You don't have to address your real situation if you can just throw the blanket of unconsciousness over the entire affair. The only problem with this, as we have said many times before, is that this much unconsciousness creates a false paradigm about your real situation. When you pray, you will find yourself praying in a way that assumes and protects this situation, without ever rectifying the larger state of affairs, which basically has to do with the conditions that produce all of this hardship in the first place.

Let us now address the factor that is most responsible for keeping all of this denial and unconsciousness in place. The ego is the main culprit, to be sure, but there are also belief systems that serve this purpose. The primary belief system that serves to reinforce the denial is the one that says that all of this is highly spiritual in nature. Again, this idea only works because of what you *don't* know about the Real World of Infinite Love. You basically have nothing to compare your situation to because it is in the nature of the finite, and the first original lie, to eclipse that truth altogether. Thus, the situation is ripe for misinterpretation. The unconsciousness is interesting, is it not? You can actually read the story of Adam and Eve, even as a metaphor, and clearly *know* that given a choice you would absolutely pick the Garden of Eden over the so-called fall. However, the level of unconsciousness does not allow this very clear fact to register, and you will continue to believe that the fall was "good" and "spiritual," even though your clear experience tells you otherwise.

If you don't like the story of Adam and Eve, that is okay. Other examples abound in your everyday life. How about the belief that strife and struggle are good things because they make you more humble and willing to learn? Well, an easier way to address the need for humility is to have no ego in the first place. Problem solved! The ego makes everything a battle. According to many spiritual tenets, this battle is in place so that you can learn. Learn what? That it's a bad idea in the first place?

One of the most interesting beliefs is that life in the finite is the only way to really feel the fulfillment of being alive. There is something about that constant state of conflict that gives one a real feeling of substance! Again, this belief is based on the fact that you have nothing to compare it to.

Let us here offer another interesting thing to contemplate. After death is seen as a place filled with peace, light, and love. It can certainly be that. It is filled with experiences as diverse and interesting as you may find when in a finite body, but there is still something missing. Otherwise, why do you keep coming back? Why do you continue to seek more? What all of these seekers are looking for is a return to their original experience of Oneness. They seek to wake up from the dream. And it will happen! The finite cannot last forever. By its very nature, it always has a beginning and an end.

So let us now discuss a brand-new way to regard your physical body. As we said before, meditation is of paramount importance. It gives you a chance to do something other than react to the circumstances surrounding you. It gives you a chance to *feel* yourself without any outside input. It gives you a chance to contemplate. See if you can allow yourself to accept the fact that you are an infinite being. Reflect on some of the things we have discussed about the ways in which you have great difficulty accepting and understanding the pitfalls and conflicts inherent in the finite. Recognize that this difficulty might actually say something good about you. It might be evidence that your heart is shouting out to you that something is wrong with this picture. And while you're at it, why not consider opening the door to your heart? Why not practice validating what your heart is trying to tell you? Why not, for a change, be true to the Truth that your heart is showing you instead of always jumping first to agree with the ego?

Once you have begun a process of practicing these things, you can allow yourself to recognize the discrepancy between what your heart is telling you about the way it's meant to be and what you experience in the finite world. You will notice that the ego always wants you to accept the negative, which reinforces your acceptance of that discrepancy. What would happen if you didn't? You might eventually find yourself able to pray a powerful and sincere prayer of commitment to the Infinite world of Love and Reality. No compromises. It is okay not to know everything about how this all works. Due to your finite situation, you are not in a position to know. It is sincerity that really matters. Remember that you are not alone!

As you become more attuned to this very different way of looking at things—where you basically seek to put the ego out of a job—you will start to get in touch with a natural love for your physical body. Why? Because you *are* love! You don't know any other experience. It is only the ego and the false identity that produce an illusion that you can feel negative. Notice that you have to be convinced by something negative first—whether it's a thought, a feeling, a circumstance, or an action—in order to feel and believe in that which is negative. It is not your natural state of being. It must always be induced.

It is highly important that you begin to cultivate a natural love for your body. Many people talk about ascension, but they have no clue about love as the only avenue to experience such a thing. Ascension is transmutation. Only love produces such an event.

You should begin by noticing how utterly unconscious you likely are inside your physical body. What produces such a profound level of unconsciousness? Primarily, it is the result of the never-ending trauma and defensiveness that occurs in that body on a daily basis, all of which is cumulative. Trauma does not have to be dramatic in order to be traumatizing. It is actually traumatizing to the nervous system to be worried on a daily basis about all the things that human beings tend to worry about. Wherever you can bring love into your entire system, it will act as a healing balm to any remnants of trauma. Wherever you can find peace in your thoughts, such peace provides a healing resonance throughout all of your cells, but it should also be remembered that Love is indeed the source of all peace.

So let us talk about the power of thought upon your entire physical embodiment. You will certainly think thoughts, but the nature of those thoughts wholly impacts your entire body, instantly, the moment that you think them. Your DNA is holographic in nature. Whenever you think a thought, it immediately lights up within the DNA of every cell. In truth, your whole body thinks because your whole body registers every single thought. Now thoughts are literally messages. They exist as electromagnetic, energy messages about the state of your reality. Your body is instantly influenced by these messages, and it immediately responds to the thought that you think. If you think that life is terrible, and all is hopeless, the body is instantly imprinted throughout its DNA with that thought. Because the DNA acts as a message center, it instantly instructs the body into a physical replica of that message. All of your atoms and molecules immediately align with whatever reality you have communicated.

Likewise, if you think a beautiful thought and truly believe it (which is key), your body is immediately uplifted, energized, and healed in multiple unseen ways. Your atoms and molecules are like a sea of rolling matter that easily conforms to whatever reality you command. This is all accomplished through electromagnetics. Remember the yin and the yang? Your thoughts are electromagnetic signals. Your atoms and molecules hold an electromagnetic charge. Due to the miracle of magnetics, they match up beautifully and create your physical reality.

Of course, this should all be very easy to do, right? Just think beautiful, positive thoughts, and everything will be great! Well, it doesn't exactly work out that way. There are many reasons for this, starting with very ancient coding in your human DNA. Remember that this entire physical body was produced as a finite manifestation with all of the fears and survival mechanisms that go with that. The body, at a very primitive level, is basically conflict oriented. Death is one of its deepest programs. The program of death is completely intertwined with sex and reproduction. They go together like hand in glove. In fact, your current lifespan is very much tied into the span of time that it takes to produce and raise offspring—and then to ensure that those offspring are fully prepared to reproduce and raise their own. Interesting, isn't it? We like to call it the recycling of souls.

In addition, you also possess the genetic programs inherited from your ancestors. Some of this is turned off, and some of it isn't, but the most important thing in this current lifetime is the ego's many interferences in your natural ability to see things in a positive way. The ego does not want you to have thoughts of love, peace, beauty, and tranquility. These thoughts are a threat to its existence. It will always attempt to override these thoughts before you ever get a chance to let them sink in. It often uses the trick of distraction, using random thoughts about meaningless, irrelevant things that make it difficult to concentrate. If you do manage to allow some beautiful thoughts to truly register, the ego will make every effort to draw your attention to something negative and change the resonating field of your cells to match its new, negative reality.

Please do not be discouraged by all of this. We are sharing this information with you so that you will have a greater understanding of what is going on. What will change this situation more than anything is the ultimate revelation that this can all be changed on a cosmic scale. But as we have repeated several times, it is important that you know what to pray for. To limit your prayers to merely asking for help in temporarily coping with any given situation, and then rationalizing that situation to the hilt—especially when you do not perceive that you have received a response—is unnecessary when you can ask for so much more. Sometimes you feel that you have not received a response to your prayers because the given reality, which is comprised of multiple elements that you cannot see, cannot accommodate the response you are asking for. It has nothing whatsoever to do with your—or anyone else's—state of worthiness. So our strong suggestion to you is to stop rationalizing, stop excusing, and learn to pray at a powerful, Universal level where you can actually suggest that you have had enough of the finite world. (And that includes the so-called Afterlife associated with it.)

So let us complete this part of the discussion with a continuation of learning to love your body. This has nothing to do with looking in the mirror and "loving" how you look. That is just more of the ego's realm of judgment. This is a love that is so much deeper and more profound. It is a love that is *felt*, not thought about. It is the purest energy of the divine. If you think that is impossible, you have already forgotten that you, yourself, are that infinite being of love. We could remind you again and again not to confuse yourself with the ego.

What we are actually talking about here is proceeding, in however small a way, to physically *occupy* your body with love because it is a part of you. The more you can occupy every cell, every molecule, and every atom with love, the more those physical elements draw closer to your infinite self. The more the body can relax and learn to live in a greater state of peace and healing, the more those elements begin to resonate with the Divine. Did you know that the higher the vibration of your thoughts, the more light and life force energy will be drawn into the body? In reality, it would be more accurate to say that the body is literally ignited with that life force energy in a beautiful, natural, graceful fashion.

One of the problems with technology is that it discourages consciousness in the physical body. Your consciousness tends to be displaced and drawn into multiple varieties of cyberspace, which actually remove life force energy from your body. Have you ever felt drained from spending too much time on the Internet?

What we are suggesting overall is that you pay close attention to the relationship that you have with your physical body. Pay attention to the fact that machines discourage that relationship; they pretend to offer you a substitute reality in their many virtual worlds. Remember that machines produce an illusion that your body is not important in their world because, in a sense, they offer themselves as a substitute body. The one shortcoming that they have in this effect, however, is that a machine can in no way accommodate your heart. They cannot give you love. They do not in any way produce health. They cannot feed you or take care of you. These are things that you must do for yourself. This may sound obvious, but there are many people who are fast losing sight of this fact. In fact, there are some who hope that someday in the future, machines—also known as robots and androids—actually *will* perform these functions for you. The hope is that you will so fall in love with these humanoid machines (in the sense that one falls in love with a new car) that you might actually want to be one yourself. There will come a day, in this lifetime or the next, when you will actually have to choose.

For now, simply remember the truth of who you are as an infinite being of love. Treat your body according to that. The infinite truth of divine love so far surpasses this finite world of machines, which masquerades as some sort of hope for your future. Take the time to experience yourself. As machines and technology cause you to feel more and more inadequate as a biological being, it will be imperative to remember who you are. Nothing in this finite world can possibly hold a candle to your magnificent, infinite self.

CHAPTER 18

The Heart

The heart is quite possibly the most mysterious part of the human experience on planet Earth. We are not talking about the physical heart. We are specifically talking about the Infinite Heart, or that which connects you directly to the Divine.

One of the first things that you should take note of is the fact that it is so mysterious. In fact, many people do not even recognize that there is such a thing. They know that they have emotions, but if you discuss the subject of the Divine Heart, they often do not know what you are talking about. If you discuss the mind, on the other hand, everybody immediately recognizes its existence—no questions asked!

It is interesting that the mind is so prominent in your experience that it can literally eclipse your experience of the heart altogether. Yet the mind functioning all by itself, with its unlimited array of ideas and perceptions, is like a very complex and large ship at sea without a captain. And this sea is stormy to boot! Do you ever feel like that in your life? Do you ever feel as though circumstances are swirling all around you, and you can't make heads or tails of what you should do?

So let us discuss the proper order of things, in terms of how you are constructed as a being. The heart is the actual core of who you are as an infinite being. It exists as your direct link to the Real World of the Divine, Infinite Love, and Truth. The heart actually has an intelligence all its own. Its intelligence is absolutely superior to that of the Earthly brain because it is based solely in the Real World of Infinite Love and expression. In other words, the heart knows the real truth about who you are as a being.

Many people misinterpret the nature of the heart and think that it is primarily about emotions and feelings. It is actually about intelligence. We like to call it the seat of the intelligence factor. Now why is this so? Try to imagine, if you will, the fact that in the infinite world of Omnipresent Love, there is only love. Everything that exists, exists as an expression of that love. Now some people think that sounds exceedingly boring. This is what I meant earlier when I said that many people believe that really *feeling* life, really feeling the *substance*, requires the conflict that is inherent in the finite. All love, all the time sounds boring!

Do you know why that is? It's because the main purpose of your life is to solve problems. What is the definition of a problem? Quite simply, a problem exists as an obstacle that is in the way of where you want to go. It is no more complicated than that. A problem will always produce conflict in your experience. That is the so-called source of substance in your life. What do you think sports are all about? You create a problem, the other team, and then you try to beat them. This only works because they are trying to beat you at the same time.

Have you ever noticed that all works of fiction, in order to be successful, *must* contain a central problem that is there to be solved? It's not that different from watching sports. It seems to be essential that there is a problem awaiting its solution in order for you to remain interested. How about self-help books? All are about different ways and methods to help you solve personal problems in your life.

Nearly every single job involves solving or avoiding problems. If your job is a cashier in a fast-food restaurant, you must solve the problem of every single customer who is hungry and wants their food now. If you don't solve that problem in an expedited way, you will have a new problem: your boss will fire you. If you are a hostess in a restaurant, you must solve the problem of where to place each customer to keep the restaurant running smoothly.

As for more complex jobs, like building a spacecraft, the entire endeavor is still all about solving problems. *How do we safely get into space in order to do the things we want to do out there?*

Look at the political arena. Every single thing that exists there involves solving some kind of problem. Suppose a person wants to run for political office. *How do I get people to know me and then vote for me?* If you are a political dictator, your problem is slightly different. *How do I hold on to my current level of power and control?*

People with health issues may ask, "How do I heal this?" For some, it might be as grave as asking, "How do I stay alive?" Problems exist in the largest spaces in your lives and in the smallest spaces. They are literally everywhere. Maybe you simply have a potted plant that is looking a little wilted. That is a problem that you must solve. *What's wrong with my plant? Is it sick? Does it need more water? Less water?* Perhaps your problem is a crying baby. *What's wrong with the baby? How can I get it to stop crying?*

Perhaps you are beginning to understand why your mind is so active! It is busy twenty-four hours a day, solving one problem after another. Even sleep is an issue. *How do I get everything done and still get enough sleep? If I don't get enough sleep, I'll be too tired tomorrow.* A dog starts barking in the middle of the night. Now that's a problem.

If you could simply step back from planet Earth for a moment and observe this in an entirely neutral fashion, you would see that this is a monumentally strange existence! The reason that you don't think it is strange is because this is all you know. Even your friends in the afterlife have a problem. Their first, most primary problem is how to communicate with you now that you can't see or hear them. Some of them even have problems like unfinished business. *You know, I really did want to live in that house just a little bit longer!* What do you think spirit-occupied houses are all about?

Have you also noticed that animals and plants all have problems that they must learn to solve every single day? Wild animals must figure out how to eat and not be eaten first. They must figure out how not to freeze to death or die of thirst. Plants must figure out how to grow and survive under ever-changing conditions.

The entire finite world is about solving and overcoming problems because of the inherent duality. A constant state of duality in existence produces a constant state of problems to be solved. In fact, your very existence is a problem in and of itself because you are an infinite being residing in a finite body.

The religions of the world have had a heyday with this situation. Their claim, across the board, is that God fully intended for this to happen. Now why would that be the case? New Age religious thought will tell you that God just wanted to have this experience. They claim that God wanted to know what it would feel like to experience pain, suffering, and death. Conceptually speaking, that can sound rather presentable, can't it? Sure it can! If you are comfortably sitting around having tea with your fellow philosophers, it's no big deal. But what if you are the person in the middle of a war who is being beheaded? While you are fully alive? They don't use anesthesia in those situations, you know.

Or how about the little child lying awake at night who is terrified of being sexually abused by a parent? How about children who witness their father violently assaulting their mother? And then being assaulted themselves? How about the excruciating pain and fear that results physically, mentally, and emotionally? Do you think it is too harsh to mention such things? Why? So that you can continue to protect your denial about this situation and go on your merry, philosophical way?

Dearest friends, if you cannot see that there is something gravely wrong with this entire picture, God help you in your future. At some point in time, you are going to have to wake up and take a position of empowerment, something you have never done before. You have excused, explained away, rationalized, justified, you name it. Why? Because you ultimately feel powerless and thus wholly intimidated.

You have been told for century upon century, millennium upon millennium, that this is all an illusion. Your saints have told you this, your scriptures have told you this, and your sages and seers have said the same. Yet you have not had the means to have this fact fully register in your consciousness. You continue to brush it off at your own peril.

Now is a time of Great Light entering your planetary realm of consciousness. You know this. It is time to take advantage of your situation and wake up to the fact that all of your explanations may have been wrong. And they have been! Reason it out for yourselves. Where do you see a solution? Where do you see change? For how long do you think this so-called God—the erroneous one that in no way matches your constant claim that this very same God is one of love—needs to continue to have this experience of death, pain, fear, torture, and violent destruction of every conceivable kind? Why can *you* not see the inherent lie in what you claim?

Now for those of you who tend to be religious in the more traditional sense of the word, what is your explanation? Is God testing you to see if you can succeed in entirely miserable conditions? Does the reward or punishment for your success or failure lie in the realm after death when you can no longer do anything about it? Does your version of God enjoy putting obstacles of every kind in your way to see how well you will do? Why? For what purpose?

You do know something about love, after all. If you love your child, is it your natural way to express that love by making it as hard on that child as you possibly can? Imagine if you were the very same God that you always talk about, in the life of that child. Well then, you would have no problem whatsoever with perhaps giving that child a terrible disease. Or letting that child starve to death in some horrible, war-torn situation. Or how about ensuring that the child grows up in poverty and terrible emotional distress? After all, if you were that God, it would all be for the good of that child, according to you. Really? How so, pray tell?

Is there any point in time, my dearest, most beloved friends, where this sort of nonsensical thinking has to stop? When? When does that moment arrive? How about right now?

This is where the subject of prayer comes in yet again. Are you sensing a theme here? If your sense of reality is completely confused, and it *is*, then your prayers will be equally confused in terms of their context. You are, without realizing it, sending very confused signals to the Universe when your heartfelt prayers arise from a belief in your own illusion. If you believe that the one true God, that of Infinite Love, has ordained pain and suffering in this Universe, then your prayers are all premised on a lie. Do you wonder why you are so confused about the unpredictable responses to your prayers? Many times, you are not even praying to the one true God. You are praying to that which ordains the physics that allow pain and suffering, agreeing with it, and then proceeding to beg for relief.

I sense that many of you have had enough, are in despair, and don't know where to turn. How can you say on the one hand, that it is by the so-called hand of a spiritual Universe of Love that every soul comes into this situation to live through, in some cases, unimaginable hell because God is all-loving, infinite grace, and would surely not want to deny *anyone* this golden opportunity? Who does this sound like to you? Does the metaphor of the serpent in the garden ring a bell? Think about it!

The Heart

I know that many of you see yourselves as lightworkers, and that may indeed be true. But here is what you must consider. If you are praying for the world out of a fundamental lie or an illusion that you insist on believing is real, how is this supposed to help? How is this profound level of compromise supposed to achieve the result you are looking for? I know that many of you pray for others, in all sincerity, whenever there is mass casualty in the form of war, natural disasters, and the like. I know that you pray wholeheartedly for the beautiful and sincere kingdom of animals and creatures of the sea. Please understand that I am in no way attempting to invalidate those prayers. Every bit of love helps, no matter how small, but I sense that many of you are ready for the "big guns," if I may use such a crass analogy. Many of you are ready for something more. Why? Because you see that it isn't working. How many sea creatures, birds, and the like that were covered in oil during your most recent oil spill had their suffering eased by your prayers? How many did not? You know, if you care to look, that millions of them died horrible deaths.

Would I be bringing all of this up if there were no answer? And more importantly, would I be bringing this up if it were true that God wanted it this way? Absolutely not. I would instead be following your false belief system and telling you how lucky those creatures were to have incarnated into such a terrible fate. Think of what they had a chance to learn! (You might notice that this learning theory doesn't hold up so well when you apply it to animals.)

What is the point of this entire discourse? It is to let you know, because you asked from within your heart of hearts, that your approach has been erroneous. Sincere, but erroneous. You are clearly ready to give something up because you have already tried everything else. My dearest, most beloved friends, you have reached a point in your evolution where merely helping yourself and those you care about is simply not enough. Why? Because it does nothing to alleviate the conditions that continue to create all of this in the first place.

I implore you to act as the gods that you truly are. To come back into living as creators who have a sense of integrity about life and Truth. Stop this deadly habit you have acquired of rationalizing and excusing, that imposes enormous weakness upon your true capabilities.

This chapter is indeed about the heart. It implores you to return to your sanity and align with that which is truly who you are. To be 100 percent present, conscious, and real. To be that which sanctions only Love. To remember your home, which contains no illusion, no lies, no suffering, and no death. Death is not the way that you get there—far from it.

When we say that the heart is the seat of real Intelligence, we say that because the heart never lies. The heart will never tell you that death is a good idea. It will never tell you that you need to suffer. It will never say that conflict and violence are good problems to have so that you can learn how to solve them. The heart will tell you the one-pointed Truth: All is really Love, and this situation that you find yourself in makes no sense, and it serves no useful purpose. Period. No compromises necessary.

Can you handle that? Or are you too afraid? If so, do not worry because we are going to discuss the source of all fear in the next chapter.

CHAPTER 19

The Source of Fear

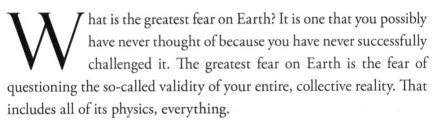

What is the greatest fear on Earth? It is one that you possibly have never thought of because you have never successfully challenged it. The greatest fear on Earth is the fear of questioning the so-called validity of your entire, collective reality. That includes all of its physics, everything.

Now what does this mean? It basically refers to everything we have been talking about so far. Let us encapsulate it so that there is no confusion. God is Eternal, Infinite, Omnipresent Love. Everything that exists in all creation exists as a pure manifestation of that Infinite Love. Period. There are no exceptions.

Now the truth is that in your current state of consciousness, you think that this sounds nice—but exceedingly boring. You subconsciously, and even consciously, believe that in such a condition of pure, infinite love, that there would be nothing to do except to just be. Thus you really have little or no motivation to exist in such a place. You continue to keep it in the background of your consciousness, but you don't *really* want to get there. Why? Because in your way of looking at it, it is rather like the goalpost at the end of the football game. Once you reach it, the game's over. In your case, you believe that if you reach that place of pure, unadulterated love, then you and your entire Universe as you know it would be over. Your erroneous view of this is that all would meld into this giant blob of "light and love," and nothing else would exist after that. What fun is that, after all?

Allow me to call into question the entire underpinnings of your overall, collective, spiritual understanding. The first clue that you could be entirely off the track is that for thousands of years you have portrayed the movements of God and the Universe in a one-dimensional, linear fashion. *God went out and separated into a whole bunch of different stars, planets, people, etc. Everything went away from God, and the whole idea is to eventually get back to God and merge back into the original state of Oneness.* That's where the giant blob of nothingness, or so-called eternal love exists in this story. The scary thing about this story, which you have been telling yourselves for millenniums, is that a whole lot of pain and suffering motivates everyone to eventually go back to God.

Now try to reason this out. If this "God" that you have created in this story were sitting around talking to itself, what would it be saying prior to this enormous saga? *Say, I have a good idea! I think I'll split myself up into a whole bunch of different parts, and then throw them away from myself. This will cause a whole bunch of problems, pain, and suffering, which will then motivate those parts of myself to eventually return to me.* Whoa! Really? Dearest friends, I ask you to reason this out with yourselves and to be truly honest. Does this actually sound believable to you? Seriously?

There are, of course, all kinds of linear variations on this theme. Some religions portray this as a gigantic, cosmic game that God plays with itself. *I think I'll create a bunch of humans, put them on Earth with every pitfall and hardship imaginable, and all kinds of pain and suffering possible. They will have no instruction manual. Then I'll have a whole bunch of different religions, giving them different sets of rules about what I really want. I'll even have them kill each other over this to cause more confusion! Then I'll punish them after death if they don't get it right, and I'll promise them rewards if they do. Of course, the odds of them getting it right will be so slim by the time I'm finished putting every conceivable obstacle in their way that only a handful will make it to heaven. The rest will likely be doomed for all eternity.* Honestly? Do you actually believe this? Friends of my dearest heart, does this not sound ever so slightly like some sort of a very strange cartoon?

The fact that all of your storylines are incredibly linear is your first clue that you are way off the track. The second clue that you are way off the track is that you believe that God would utilize fear and pain as a motivating force for anything! The third clue is that the way you have portrayed your so-called goal of merging back into Oneness is so boring that even God itself would probably fall asleep.

The fact, my dearest friends, is that you literally have no idea what you're talking about! That is not meant to be an insult. My intention is only to clear the path of all of these erroneous assumptions. Certainly you have already had many thousands of years to test these theories out. The real question is whether you are ready to let go of them yet. Where is the evidence that any of this is real? Have you ever thought of that?

It is not that you must take my word for any of this. Your heart is your true seat of Knowledge and Love. If you learn to pay attention to it and assign it far more credibility than you already have, you might be very surprised by what you learn.

Let us now discuss what I will term the ultimate and highly scientific, true source of the existence of fear itself. What is the actual definition of fear? Quite simply, it is the literal experience of being separated from Infinite, Omnipresent Oneness or God. The mistake in your previous explanation for this is that God intentionally created this separation for a purpose. That is your mistake.

First of all, it must be said that this experience of separation is an illusion. It is simply not possible, on any level, to be separate from Omnipresent Oneness. If that is so, then where does this experience of separation come from? Well, that is indeed the first brilliant question that you are capable of asking!

Let us go back again to the story of the first, original lie. The lie called "I am *not* Omnipresence. I am *not* Infinite." Put another way, it says, "I am *not* Love." This simple lie, which manifested, most definitely produced a very definite result in terms of physics. Let me explain. But before I do, I sense that there are some people who have a question, so allow me to respond to that first.

How is it possible for God to create such a lie in the first place? God did not create such a lie. This lie only exists as a potentiality, albeit one that could never manifest in truth. That is precisely what makes it an illusion, you see. You may not understand the subject of potentialities because you appear to be trapped inside one at this particular time in space. Even that is tricky to talk about because time itself is a grand illusion. In the meantime, it may be more effective for you to exercise your ability to sense things that exist at a higher level than what your current brain's structure can allow you to comprehend. At the present time, however, it is not necessary for you to know everything there is to know about such things.

So let us talk about what is important to know. The logistics of this first, original lie are really rather simple. In the Real World of Omnipresent Love and Infinite Truth, everything that manifests and therefore exists, exists as a statement of what it *is*. What do you think that ultimately is? Infinite Love, of course. You do not see that manifesting in the finite world. Why not? Because the moment that you introduce the lie of "I am *not*," you are essentially saying that something can be known by what it *isn't*, which is, of course, impossible. This is the reason that everything in the finite world exists in a state of pure and perfect mathematical division.

Did you know that all of mathematics must start with division? The first act of division was created by the first original lie. When you say, "I am *not* Omnipresence," you have for the first time created two things instead of one. The original *one* is infinite. All-encompassing. To say, "I am *not* that" is a lie that says you are something else, which is, of course, impossible. That is what makes it an illusion—get it?

So now, in that lie, the entire Universe appears at its core as two things instead of one. The entire experience is now an illusion. A virtual dream. In this dream, there appear to be two things: God and I am *not* God. Infinite and I am *not* Infinite. Love and I am *not* Love. Do you see how silly and pointless this ultimately is? The problem with this lie is that in the illusion that it produces there does not appear to be anything whatsoever that is Infinite. The idea of Infinite changes into a numerical factor and is perceived as a condition of unlimited numbers, all of which represent things that are separate from one another. The entire Universe now exists as a numerical manifestation. This is only one example of the new laws of physics that get created by this lie. And it does create physics. Make no mistake about that! Dare I say that your scientists can only busy themselves with studying the physics of this first original lie?

As far as the Infinite God is concerned, there is no infinite god in the finite world. Why do you think you can't see or know this creator? Is it because it is hiding from you? Of course not. Remember that in this illusion, there are now two things, instead of one. Neither of these two things is real; therefore, God has now become a mere concept. Something with defined lines. Where do you think the idea of the man in the sky with the white beard came from? You have to find some way to identify that which you cannot see or feel. It is interesting that this illusion of a man in the sky is portrayed as someone who judges everyone as good or bad, right or wrong. Of course! This is the god of the ultimate duality created by what I will now refer to as the source of fear.

Once this original lie is well in place, which is virtually in an instant, it creates the finite. The finite is that which is termed "*not* infinite." If that were possible (which it isn't), it would mean that there is no such thing as infinite. The "I am *not*" resists the truth of the Infinite, thereby creating an illusionary reality where all is finite—and everything exists in separation from everything else. All things in that reality are known by what they are *not*; thus, everything is inherently a threat to the identity of everything else. Thus you have war, conflict, division, and separation, and all of the pain and suffering that goes along with that.

The apparent division from God creates the greatest pain. This is the reason that it is so easy to have so many different religions, all of which conflict with one another in some way or another. Even the God that you think you're divided from is not real! Can you get that? It is not possible to be divided from the True, Infinite God. In your grand illusion, there is God on one side of the fence, and you are on the other. You pray to this God, hoping that he/she/it will have mercy on you, and hoping that you will be heard.

For those who feel a true connection to God, let me say this. This is where your true heart of hearts comes into play. This one, true heart, as I've said before, is absolutely at One with Reality. The problem is that you are so distracted and confused by all that exists in the duality of the finite that you rarely, if ever, connect with it. It has been reduced to a mere shadow of an experience that lives primarily in the background of your everyday life. In most cases, it remains completely unconscious. When you actually feel that real connection, it is because you may have stumbled upon waking up to the fact that you are actually, *permanently*, connected to that truth. What you need now is to become One with it. You need to wake up from the dream.

For those who believe that death is the moment at which you wake up, I am sad to inform you that it isn't. How can I say that?

Quite simply, if you are experiencing something called death, you are still existing in the very same illusion. As I said before, the Afterlife is directly connected to the finite. You are still dealing with a duality of being alive and *not* alive. You are still residing in a Universe of being here and *not* here. This should not depress you if you have loved ones residing in what you call "the other side." There are many "other sides" in the finite Universe. They exist all over the place in your everyday life, for heaven's sake. You are all ultimately sharing the very same reality.

Have you noticed how much you long for the presence of those whom you love, who have already passed over? Do you think there is something wrong with you for feeling this way? Of course there isn't! You and they will continue to have this longing to be together in the stable Universe where all is Infinite, and there is no such thing as separation and "other sides." If it is any comfort to you, know that you and your loved ones absolutely share the Truth of the Infinite Real World. Whether you know it or not, you both (or all) reside there together right now. You are currently sharing a mutual dream of separation, and you will absolutely awaken from this shared illusion. In fact, you are already awake! You just don't know it from where you sit in the finite.

Now let us talk specifically about the source of fear. The lie of "I am *not*" produces an immediate absence of precisely what it is that you are not. If what you are *not* is God, if what you are *not* is Infinite, if what you are *not* is Love, you will ultimately experience an absence of those things and ultimately an absence of your *self*. The experience of this absence is what you call *fear*. Fear is simply an experience of the so-called *absence* of God. Since this is impossible, the experience is an illusion.

I must caution you about something here. There are those who would wish to stop at this point and suggest that the simple answer whenever you feel fear is to simply remind yourself that it is merely an illusion. Ta-da! Problem solved. Well, not exactly. Try it if you don't believe me.

The source of fear, which is the first, original lie, creates a boatload of physics. Your finite DNA is deeply embedded with those physics, as is everything else around you in the finite Universe. In fact, fear is the life's blood of the ego. Thus, you are literally living the proverbial battle of Armageddon in your everyday life. You live that battle every time you feel anger, every time you allow the ego to intimidate you, and every time you allow the ego to intimidate or judge others.

The goal in this discourse is to provide you with the opportunity to see if you are truly fed up with all of this. Why? Because when you are truly fed up, when you stop making excuses, when you stop blaming all of this on so-called guilty humans, or blaming it on God, the devil, or whatever other fantasy you may harbor, you will be left with facing the actual experience itself. You will have the opportunity to exhibit genuine intolerance.

Intolerance does not mean conflict in the sense that it is being used here. It means a state where you are truly connected with your own heart. It means that you have finally reached the Mother Ship that you have so desperately been seeking. The Mother Ship is by no means a physical ship in outer space. Good heavens, no! (I'm very familiar with that idea, by the way.) That "Mother Ship" is in actuality the lifeline to the Real World that is always present, always with you. It is your most precious, divine, human heart. It is that which no one can take away from you. You may lose touch with it, but it is always there. You are permanently at one with the Infinite Love of God.

The intolerance that I am referring to occurs when you experience and are true to your very own, infinite heart of Love. It occurs when you listen to what your heart has been trying to tell you for eons. That you are *right* when you feel that there should be no death. That you are *right* when you want to experience only peace. That you are *right* when you feel that all should be love, forever and ever. The only thing that will ever tell you that you are wrong is the ego, which exists as the virtual agent for the source of fear itself.

Let me address the subject that I brought up earlier when I said that the finite does not allow you to experience the truth about Omnipresent Oneness and Infinite Love. The *absence* of Love, which is fear, only allows you to have a conceptual knowing of what this Omnipresent Love is. Because you don't experience it since the thing that is the most real to you is the finite, you erroneously perceive that there is nothing there but a "blob" of love that goes on forever. You erroneously believe that if the problem of separation is solved, and all has returned to a state of so-called oneness with this blob of love, then there will be nothing more to do. Basically what this really translates into is a state of nothingness in your imagination. Therefore, you are not interested. You might be suffering now, but at least there's something going on, for heaven's sake! Who wants to merge with a blob and do absolutely nothing after that? There are more specific reasons for why things appear this way, but that will have to be saved for another time. For the purposes of this discussion, this is what is most important for you to know.

Do not underestimate the power of the erroneous perception that I just described to entirely circumvent your will to eliminate this predicament of separation that you find yourselves in. It is nearly impossible to call up sufficient will from within yourself if you have a perception that solving the real issue will mean that you cease to exist in the "oneness" of the blob. On another occasion, I will explain what that really means, but for now, here is a clue. The only thing that will cease to exist, for sure, is your ego. You will remain fully intact, fully whole. Don't try to figure that out right now. For now, intolerance born of the heart is the main, first step.

Let's address the issue of intolerance to make sure that you are really clear about what that means. Have you ever had an injury or an illness that caused you great strife and that you were not able to initially heal? Perhaps you tried everything you knew to accept that predicament and make the best of it because it fit in with your identity on some subconscious level. You may have become exceedingly frustrated when you realized the limitation that this physical situation was imposing on you. At that point, a person can sometimes reach a crossroads in their consciousness.

Many people come to terms with the situation by accepting it and reworking their identities to include it. This is fine, if that is your choice, but some will choose to evolve out of that particular expression of identity. They will feel in their hearts that such situations are intolerable, and that expanding their ability to function is more important. They conclude that they simply cannot accommodate this thing in their lives any longer. This does not necessarily happen on a conscious level. It cannot be forced. It has more to do with who you are in terms of your own evolution and purpose. The intolerance that is experienced is not one of frustration. It is never born of conflict with the situation itself. It is more a sense of resolve that is not accompanied by effort. It exists, in truth, as a paradigm shift in consciousness. There is simply not room in the new paradigm for this predicament to continue to exist.

What usually follows is a solution to the problem. This can come in the form of a treatment that was heretofore unknown to the person, a treatment that is ultimately successful. All manner of aid will often show up, and the person may marvel that this didn't happen before. The aid is often attributed to God or to answered prayers. In a manner of speaking, this may be true, but there is a lot more to it than that. These things do not happen in an environment of fear. Fear is the most debilitating part of the entire picture because fear is literally the experience of an illusion that you are completely separated from God.

This is why, at the end of the last chapter, I asked if you were afraid to listen to your heart and truly accept what it has always been trying to tell you. The ego does not want you to ever listen to your heart. It will belittle it and convince you that it is of no consequence. It will tell you it is dangerous to listen to something that doesn't understand or agree with the finite principles of the finite Universe.

The ego lives in fear of its own demise. Its entire motivating force is survival. That is why it finds a finite body so well suited to its finite self. The body, too, lives only to survive. Its entire programming is to try to stay alive, no matter what. This is why the ego's greatest fear is for you, in your true self, to cease sanctioning death as an important spiritual experience. The finite body and the ego are perfectly suited for one another. They both exist in mortal fear of their own destruction. The body's chemical composition is specifically structured to avoid death. It's fight-or-flight reaction patterns are there for exactly the same purpose. The drive to reproduce is precisely tied into this need to survive. It is the only way to have death and life exist in the same reality.

Let us complete this part of things by discussing the Reality behind this massive Universal illusion. Contrary to the ego's need for you to see that reality as a seeming blob of "Oneness" where nothing really happens because all is love, the Real World is vastly different. Do you think that the Infinite God does not create infinite being-ness? There are multiple Universes of Infinite life. There is no way for you to comprehend what happens there in your currently divided state. It is simply not within your current realm of consciousness to know. But suffice it to say that pain, suffering, death, and illusion do not exist in that Real World of Truth and Infinite Love.

One of the hallmarks of the ego is to convince you that all there is to know should be known by you in your finite state. But this is delusional, if you think about it. All you can know in the finite is that which is finite. All you can know in your current state of consciousness is that which exists in that very same state of consciousness. Can you possibly recognize that even this finite Universe is far too expansive to exist only for the purpose of accommodating the potential knowledge of one very tiny species on one very tiny planet?

If the gargantuan nature of all of this overwhelms you, do not allow yourself to be distressed. Please remember that your simple, divine heart of hearts is *always* connected to—and is at one with—the Infinite Love that creates all that is real. You can never be lost. You can always be at peace in knowing that nothing can ever remove you from that Truth. If you were aware enough, you would know that you could relax at any time in the sheer tranquility of this experience. It's called surrender. But in order to have surrender, you must first have awareness. And more than anything else, that awareness needs to lead to a sincere surrender in knowing that it is okay not to know everything because you are already connected to all that matters.

Remember that all you really want is love. Not the love of this finite reality, which is always fickle at best. What you want and need is a conscious experience of the True and Infinite Love of God. In fact, what you really desire is to *be* that Love. This is the true security that you seek, and I am here to tell you that you have it.

CHAPTER 20

Conclusion

So here we are, my dearest friends, at what we shall call the conclusion of this discourse. Now this may seem unusual since there is indeed one more chapter to go. But conclusion, in this sense, means something different than what you are used to. In this case, we are referring to an opportunity to assemble all the understanding that has been provided here and allow it to synthesize in your consciousness. The purpose of this synthesis is to provide you with an opportunity to make a powerful shift to an entirely new level of consciousness. In other words, we wish to offer you an opportunity to move your being and your consciousness to an altogether new platform, one upon which you have never resided before.

You have spent many thousands of years trying to resolve the duality produced by the first, original lie. The lie called "I am *not* Infinite," "I am *not* Eternal Love," and ultimately "I am *not* God." Have you realized by now that there is no resolution to this duality? There is no amount of time that will pass, no amount of trying, no amount of good deeds, and no amount of finite love that will eliminate the problems caused by the phenomenon produced by this first, original lie, and all the physics that it manifests. That is not meant to exist as a negative idea. It literally describes what you have been collectively living for as long as you have been aware of human existence on planet Earth.

Let us discuss where your mistake has been and how you can correct it. With all sincerity, you have tried with all your heart to bring enough love into this world to somehow allay the suffering that exists here. There is certainly nothing wrong with that, and without question, it is much appreciated and needed by all. We encourage you to continue! But as you witness more and more events overtaking your efforts, you are surely at a place of wanting more. I have come to assist you with understanding what that something more is.

Let us begin by clearly identifying the usual perspective that is exercised by those who desire to help. In some ways, it helps to view this situation through a mathematical lens in order to see clearly what is going on. Imagine that you have a board, something akin to a game board. At the center of this board, there is a microscopic black hole. At the center of this hole, there is a strange, invisible phenomenon. This phenomenon exists as the Source of Fear. It is literally an energetic manifestation of the first, original lie. This phenomenon creates a field of energy throughout the surrounding platform of the game board. This field of energy immediately distorts the *real* reality of that board, which is that everything exists as what it *is*—and turns it into an illusion where everything appears to exist as what it is *not*. As a result of this, an illusion of duality is created across this entire board. Everything exists in conflict with everything else. All things that exist on this board have to negotiate their existence with everything else. Harmony does not occur naturally since all things vie for their most optimal position of survival.

Now if this board were a planet, there would be people who existed as a part of its overall environment. These people would experience this illusion every single day, and they would watch themselves try to negotiate their ongoing survival and existence as they continued to try to maintain themselves in this environment where they had to continuously prove to themselves that they *are* what they are apparently *not* in this illusion. They would experience that life is difficult and painful. Happiness would require tremendous effort because they would have to work at it and remind themselves of it every day. They would have to do affirmations all day long and try to remind themselves to think positively since the ever-encroaching "I am *not*" would continuously conflict with that happiness.

Somewhere deep inside, they would know that something was very wrong. "Happiness should be a given," their hearts would whisper to them. Everyone should be loved. Life should not be so hard. And why do we have to work so hard to maintain joy?

They would witness those who could not manage this succumb to the despair of their overwhelming circumstances. Feeling guilty, they learn to pray for those others and do whatever they can to help. Some would make it their life's purpose to bring relief to those who could not withstand the onslaught of devastating circumstances that would enter their lives for some inexplicable reason. Overall, it would be like a constant war of good versus evil. Evil mysteriously seemed to maintain the upper hand as wars raged and people died. Poverty was the global norm, starvation was rampant, disease developed over and over again, and people simply degraded into accepting their fates.

Desperate for some explanation in order to maintain their psychological survival, the people would begin to tell themselves stories about how this was really a *good* thing on some unseen, spiritual level. They would be subtly influenced due to the overwhelming influence of their illusion and begin lying to themselves. They would tell themselves that this was really good and that it existed as an opportunity to learn and appreciate that which they did not have. "Learning through the negative consequences of our innocent mistakes is necessary and good," they would say. What better way to learn than through the inherent nature of this unusual reality where positive and negative consequences served as a built-in system of reward and punishment?

They would undergo depression and work very hard to find solutions to that predicament, all the while telling themselves that everything was really okay; they just needed to learn to appreciate what they had. Some would say that the hardship was punishment for wanting too much. "No one really needs that much," they would say. Guilt would be the word of the day!

Some of these people would figure out that this duality and all of its accompanying hardship was being created by something. They would assume in the unconsciousness of their illusion that it had to be their God. After all, they would think, this is all we know. It would therefore be assumed that this *was* the entire Universe of creation. So they would pray to their God for mercy and help. "Please make our lives easier!" they would say.

But what they wouldn't know is that the invisible phenomenon at the center of this board couldn't do anything else but continue to produce more of the same. They would not realize that there could be no other outcome from the first, original lie. They would not understand that it was all due to the laws of physics produced by that phenomenon.

Yet all the while, their *true* hearts would be speaking to them. Their true hearts would be whispering that it wasn't meant to be this way. *No one should ever suffer and die, and God is really Infinite Love.* In their confusion and desperate struggle to survive, they would doubt what their true heart was telling them. *Where is the evidence?* Seeing none, they would say to themselves, "No, no. This is clearly wrong. I am obviously imagining things, and no good can come out of this feeling."

They would bury it and go on with seeking ways to balance the bad with the good. They would somehow get by. If that didn't work, there was always lying to themselves. Why not? When you are breathing in an atmosphere of lies, what's the big deal? Lying, against your heart, is pretty much part of the status quo. It is, after all, the only way to integrate with this illusion.

Over time, however, all of these various coping mechanisms would begin to wear thin. War and violence would continue to rage. Poverty and starvation would not abate. Abuse of all living things would continue. The people would begin to pray more deeply as they realized that their excuses, denial, and "spiritual" explanations were weakening in their effects. They would grow more and more sincere. They would begin to recognize that they really didn't know.

The angels would hear. The sincere need for an answer would draw those angels out of their veiled existence in the people's illusion. They would begin to come forth through that veil with their divine hands extended in Love. The people would begin waking up as they learned to listen—maybe for the first time—to the quiet song in their hearts. The song would at first seem far away, but the more the people listened, the louder and clearer that song would grow. It was the music of the spheres ... a choir of angels ... a message from home! Their True home in Infinite Love. *But we thought it was far away!* The people would be surprised and even shocked that that connection was within them all along.

The angels would come and speak to them about their plights. The angels would marvel that the people's questions had changed! No longer were they asking for ways to help them cope. No longer would they ask for the angels to bandage their wounds as they remained on a battlefield that they assumed would never end. No longer were they asking the angels to help them learn to accept the dying of loved ones— and ultimately the loss of their own lives.

There was a new light emerging in this god-forsaken place! The light of consciousness. The light of Truth. The people had been listening for eons to all of the reasons why they needed to be in this predicament. They were tired. They wanted to listen to something else.

This is where we are today, my dearest, most beloved friends. If this example describes your feelings, then we are ready to take you to a brand-new platform of evolution. On this brand-new platform of consciousness, you can actually *see* what is really going on here. When you can see the truth of your situation rather than being mesmerized by the illusion, you will indeed begin to pray in a completely new way. You will find it impossible not to pray for the whole, in addition to yourself, because you will realize that it is all the very same situation. Your vision will automatically change, and you will begin to know exactly what you should do. You will understand to set your sights on *home*, pure and simple. Home is not a physical place that you must travel to in some sort of spaceship that takes you off this planet. It most certainly is not where you go after you die.

It is a beautiful place of a reality that is so real, so amazing, so perfect, and so incredibly free. In that place, you breathe only Life. There is no such thing as fear because all is known by what it *is*—and never by what it is not. This home is so *real* that it exposes your current reality as the distant and vague illusion that it truly is. It exposes the dream, the vacantness where you search for God but never find.

We angels are here to help you, but we can only help you to the degree that you sincerely want it. First, you must be willing to listen to your heart. Your heart already knows the Truth. It is what keeps you in that home even now when you are sound asleep.

It is important to know that there are not enough prayers in the old world of your previous consciousness, where you merely ask for assistance in coping, and in helping others to cope. You cannot possibly cover all the bases of all the suffering—human, animal, Earth, and plant, but you already know this because you have tried it so many times. That original source of fear, that original lie, will continue to churn out the same results—no matter how many prayers you pray in this regard.

We offer you an opportunity to pray for something else. To pray from a different place. A new perspective. Why is it that we continue to mention prayer? Because prayer exists as your Divine right to exercise your Infinite will as an extension of Omnipresent Love. You have not been praying from this place. Instead, you continue to pray from within the dream, as though you are a part of the dream itself. This means that in your mind, in your subconscious need to survive in this illusion, you are sending a signal to preserve the dream and to help you to cope.

Is this what your heart truly wants? Or does your heart beckon you again and again to wake up because none of this should exist in your experience in the first place?

We do not expect you to know how to wake up on your own. You are still far too entrenched in the dream. But your heart is now awake, collectively and individually. There is light emerging in your consciousness. The dawn is near.

CHAPTER 21

Light

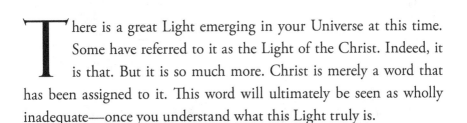

There is a great Light emerging in your Universe at this time. Some have referred to it as the Light of the Christ. Indeed, it is that. But it is so much more. Christ is merely a word that has been assigned to it. This word will ultimately be seen as wholly inadequate—once you understand what this Light truly is.

This Light is what some have referred to as the Light of the Father. The Light of the Creator. In truth, it is the Light of God itself. It is the Light that shines ever so brightly in the Real World of which I speak.

You do not know what is behind this Light, but you will. This Light is so powerful—and so filled with Love—that it influences the frequency of your entire Universe. Perhaps you have felt it as a quickening of sorts.

This Light is the light that exists within your hearts. You don't know it yet because that Light has been eclipsed by the source of fear. The first, original lie, which all who live in this finite Universe experience uniformly and collectively is what keeps you and everything you know locked within the dream. Now that your hearts are collectively awakening from their deep and ancient slumbers, that Light is touching all of you. We angels want to encourage you to begin to wake up. The Light of this gentle dawning of Love shall cause you to remember.

You may think that there is much hard work to do in order to correct your situation here. It is only because that is all you have ever known. You have tried to solve everything alone because alone is how you have felt. I have come to tell you that you are not alone; soon you will realize that for yourselves.

Do not try to force this awakening. No flower is ever served by ripping open its petals before their time. Allow this gentle Light of Love and Infinite Power to effortlessly coax your heart awake. In the same way that the early morning sun ever so gently shows its light at the edge of Earth's horizon and gradually awakens all of life, allow this Infinite Light to apply its subtle touch of Love and reassurance.

You will ultimately not be able to resist this incredible Light and the clarity it brings, just as you cannot resist the physical sight of morning's glory as the sun spreads its light across the land.

Let me now forewarn you about some things that you can expect, lest these things confuse you and cause you to doubt the Truth that is in your heart.

The source of fear, or the principle known as the first, original lie, is a phenomenon based on resistance. The more that the Infinite expands in its radiating flow of celestial beauty and Love, the more this phenomenon will resist that Truth in order to continue its survival. Its survival is wholly dependent upon its ability to continue the lie that it is *not* any of this. Eventually, this phenomenon will deplete itself of all its energy. One can only remain "*not* infinite" for so long. Its dying Universe of illusion will eventually expire when this erroneous so-called creation fails to be able to maintain the facade.

There are powerful forces of nature and evolution in the Real World of Infinite Light and Love that have already come to your assistance. As these forces of Light act upon your situation, you will witness the death throes of this enormous beast. You will see its last-ditch efforts to intimidate you and convince you that it is more real than Love. You will witness this in the form of war, hunger, and the dire consequences of its total infiltration in your overall experience. You will see death all around you while this beast does everything in its power to prove that it does exist. But fear not death, my beloved friends—your own or anyone else's—for as I've told you that it is *all* an illusion, including the so-called afterlife. Nothing shall escape the Light as it illuminates all that is not real and causes it to disintegrate into the nothingness from which it came.

If this sounds frightening or intimidating to you, I ask you to remember that you are already living this today. In fact, you have been living this for thousands of years while human beings have continued to slaughter, torture, and destroy themselves and all that lives around them. Remember that what I have said to you is certainly nothing new.

And now let us discuss your role in this amazing drama. If you have been reading this illustrious book, you must certainly consider yourself a lightworker. At the very least, you may have been curious about it.

Your first role shall always be that of Love for yourself, your neighbors, your family, and your friends. Love for life itself, in all of its forms. Please remember that when I say all of its forms, I am only referring to the Truth of what life really is. It should never be confused with that which is "anti-life," simply because it is there.

Most of you already understand the importance of Love as the basis of all else that you may do in order to serve this situation, but let us now address the context for that Love so that you are able to enact a powerful paradigm shift in terms of how you see it.

Prior to now, you have seen an act of Love as a way to help yourself and others cope with each other's individual situations, but you have never effectively questioned the existence of the situation itself. I would now like to provide you with a brand-new context for that Love. This planet, this Universe, and all of its inhabitants are on the verge and in the process of going through a massive transformation and transition into what will ultimately manifest as a gargantuan wake-up call. It will be difficult for some people. There will be people, animals, and plants on this planet that will require enormous levels of help. Rather than seeing your Love as a balm to help them cope, try to see it as a powerful support for their own individual awakening.

You do not have to say anything about this in words. In fact, it is sometimes better if you don't, lest it be reduced to a mere concept or belief system. Rely instead on the power of your own experience. Rely instead on the power of your enhanced vibration as a result of that experience. Allow the laws and principles of resonance to do their work as your vibratory field of knowingness influences that other person's consciousness in a wholly positive way.

When you are secure in that knowingness—and you vibrate in unison with that ultimate Truth that lives outside of this artificial realm of duality and illusion—you exist as an energy of peace. Your vibration communicates with absolute perfection the reality of that Truth in a way that words can never hope to touch. The power of that vibration will touch that person's heart with a knowing remembrance of Infinite Love and Tranquility. This is what people really need to feel. This is the hope that will contribute to individual awakening. Be a silent angel.

For those of you who are already engaged in work of a higher order, which is intended to heal and protect this planetary sphere, raise your consciousness to a much higher level of Love and Light. Give up the belief that you are all in this mess together, and you are therefore going to help others in the context of the mess itself. See if you have the courage to be different. See if you have the fortitude to make a difference from a higher platform of experience. Again, you do not have to be able to talk about this directly. You can continue to do your work in the same basic way, but never underestimate the absolute power of any human being to influence the outcome when that human being is awake and aware of what is really going on, when that human being understands the difference between what is illusion and what is real.

And most of all, take good care of yourself. You are not by any means a dispensable person. You are greatly needed. You are enormously appreciated for your sincere willingness to try. I and all others who care about this beautiful Earth love you deeply for all of your efforts. Do not be discouraged whenever you feel that you may have failed. Instead, forgive yourself. Remind yourself that the appearance of failure is merely another symptom of why you are so committed in the first place.

Whenever you feel that you want to cry because it may all seem so overwhelming, remember that there are many who have cried before you. There are many who forgot to seek solace in the comfort of their own Eternal Heart. You can change that. You can remember.

And above all, remember that you are not alone. Your heart is filled with Love, and it is always there to comfort you, inspire you, and give you hope. All you have to do is listen. Some may find that impossible to understand, particularly if they are filled with fear. If that is the case, find a quiet place. Play some music that tends to evoke a feeling of serenity and tranquility. Listen to the angels as they gently strum your heart. Remind yourself that if you are afraid, it is because something is telling you in that moment that fear is all there is. Your body is programmed to instantly react to fear to ensure its survival, but you are an Infinite Being. You have no worries whatsoever about things such as survival. Remember that fear is only a sensation. A chemical reaction in the body. It is like the worst drug you could ever ingest.

Now take some very deep breaths. Notice how your breath mimics the wave action of Earth's beautiful oceans. Even the sound of your breath moving in and out is very similar to that of the sea as its waves gently caress the shore. Feel the tranquility of this beautiful, eternal motion as it plays out again and again in your own body, reminding you of the Joy of Infinite Life. Reminding you of the yin and the yang of all creation. See your breath as the gateway to your heart. Tell your body that everything is okay as you open the door to your eternal presence. Listen to what your heart wants to tell you without the filter of your thinking mind. Let your mind rest as you bathe in the Light of your Eternal Self. There is no "higher" self anymore. Your whole self is here with you right now. The self that is already home.

Now let that self tell you what that home is like. Let it describe to you the ineffable beauty, the brilliant color, and the color of every softness and hue. Let it describe to you a world without fear, and most importantly, know that this is *true*. Allow the peace of this understanding to wash over you like a soothing balm of hope to your formerly battered consciousness. A consciousness that thought that the only thing that existed was the perpetual battle to survive.

If you find it difficult to imagine that you could do all of this, remember that the source of that apparent difficulty lies in the fact that you have never listened. Your habit has been to shut down what your Infinite Heart is trying to tell you out of a fear that it could be wrong. Out of a fear that it might destroy the entire world of your illusion. And it would. And you would therefore be happy for the first time. What is really afraid of this destruction? Only that which has created the illusion of destruction in the first place.

And finally, remember your angels. Remember your friends. There are powerful forces throughout this Real Universe who love you. Who are always there for you. We ask that you meet us where we live. Why? Because it is also where you live, if you could only remember. There is no fear here. Only Love.

I adore you, and I Bless you for all Eternity.

Your Beloved Archangel Michael

EPILOGUE

Beloved friends of Earth,
We are here to aid you, and forever have we loved you from afar.
Be not in distress as you witness your planetary sphere seeming to
Fail all around you.
Your real planet Earth, the paradise that you seek, awaits.
Come home.
Come home and witness the truth of who you are.
See the ineffable joy of the real Universe that lives in Love.
Awaken from your millennia-old slumber.
Awaken from your dream of death and destruction, none of which
Truly exist.
Call upon us whenever you need reminding.
Call on us whenever you need Love.
We are your Inter-Universal friends and comrades.
We are here for you.
To the Light, forever and ever!
Our eternal blessings are yours to keep.
We adore who you are, and we adore why you are here.
Beloved Ones,
We await you.

—Archangel Michael and your beloved angels

ABOUT THE AUTHOR

Saratoga Ocean is the founder and creator of Telstar Events. Telstar is an evolutionary, cosmic force of nature represented by six channeled beings who are individually named Adam, Isadora, Sangia, John, Mikhail, and Miribi. The name "Mikhail" is the one used by Archangel Michael for purposes of Telstar's communication. Saratoga has been the exclusive channel for Telstar for over twenty-five years.

Saratoga entered planet Earth as a "walk-in" in order to represent Telstar and function as their channel. She and Telstar have produced numerous events designed to help people reach their greatest potential and evolve into a universe of infinite Love. Their signature event is entitled *The Final Elimination of the Source of Fear*. This powerful event was created by Archangel Michael and Telstar. It was originally presented as a live event in cities across North America. The exact same process in now available in Saratoga's book by the same title.

Telstar's events are available online at *SaratogaOcean.com* as programs and processes that can be done at home to accelerate your personal growth and amplify your ability to reach your goals. All of Telstar's events and programs have a powerful, transformational effect when approached with a sincere heart. In addition to Telstar's work,

Saratoga also partners with angels and has been certified by Doreen Virtue, PhD, as an Angel Therapy Practitioner.

To learn more about Saratoga and Telstar, visit their website at *SaratogaOcean.com*. Sign up there for Saratoga's mailing list and receive free gifts and free ongoing support.

We have something special just for you...

To receive special gifts, resources, and exclusive offers for readers of *A Guide for Lightworkers*, visit **AGuideforLightworkers.com/resources** or scan the code below with your mobile device.

For daily inspiration, guidance, and tips to help you create the life you want, connect with Saratoga on social media:

Facebook.com/SaratogaOcean
Twitter @SaratogaOcean
Instagram @saratoga.ocean
Pinterest.com/SaratogaOcean

Discover more books and products from Saratoga and Telstar, and read Saratoga's blog, at

www.SaratogaOcean.com

CPSIA information can be obtained
at www.ICGtesting.com
Printed in the USA
FSHW011305010621
81971FS